THE OLD
TRAIL TO SANTA FE

THE OLD
TRAIL TO SANTA FE

Collected Essays

MARC SIMMONS

UNIVERSITY OF NEW MEXICO PRESS
ALBUQUERQUE

Library of Congress Cataloging-in-Publication Data

Simmons, Marc.
    The old trail to Santa Fe : collected essays / Marc Simmons.—1st ed.
      p.   cm.
    Includes bibliographical references (p.).
    ISBN 0-8263-1726-X (c). — ISBN 0-8263-1737-5 (p)
    1. Santa Fe Trail—History. I. Title.
F786.S57   1996
978—dc20   96-26016
                                     CIP

To the
Officers and Members of the
Santa Fe Trail Association

for their dedication
to the history of the old trail

CONTENTS

ILLUSTRATIONS

PREFACE

"How can you have a love affair with an old trail?" I am often asked. The question comes from friends who know that for years I have been smitten with the Santa Fe Trail.

Truth to tell, the whys and wherefores of the matter are not easily answered. When pressed for an explanation, I am at a loss to account for my infatuation. In part it can probably be attributed to the aura of magic and enchantment which seems to cling to every blood-stained, dusty, history-laden segment of the trail's thousand-mile length.

Some of my fondness, too, has grown from familiarity. I have made numerous round-trip drives by auto over the Santa Fe Trail. And smaller sections of it I have hiked or ridden horseback.

Early-day travelers frequently discovered that by their second or third journey to Santa Fe they had become firmly wedded to trail life. The wide and uncluttered vistas, the dazzling sunsets, the smell of buffalo or antelope steaks roasting on a campfire, and the first taste of sweet mountain water as the wagon caravans neared the outliers of the Rockies all exerted their appeal.

As an observant Josiah Gregg phrased it in the 1840s: "The trail experience begat a fierce passion for prairie travel." Another man of that same decade, C. B. Gillespie, wrote nostalgically upon his return from a trip over the Santa Fe road: "There is charm in such a life, which, when the journey is past and the traveler sits himself down once more amongst the pleasures of his home, will draw his mind back with fond regret, creating sad longings which will linger as fancy may be suffered to dwell upon the past."

I believe that anyone who succumbs to the modern charms of Santa Fe, and in the process learns a bit of her history, must sooner or later arrive at an understanding of how the old trail from Missouri transformed New Mexico's capital and, building upon its rich Hispanic tradition, helped create a municipality that today bears the indelible stamp of its own past.

For there can be no debate that Santa Fe would now be a very different place had not the famous trail that took her name flourished at the time and in the way that it did. I reflect upon that historical truth every time I stop and pay my respects to the End-of-the-Trail Monument that sits on the southeast corner of the Santa Fe plaza, opposite La Fonda Hotel.

The face of the chest-high granite monument has a smooth polish and bears a historical inscription as well as an incised map of the two western branches of the trail—the

Cimarron Cutoff and the Mountain Route. When the marker was unveiled in 1910, half of Santa Fe turned out for the brass band ceremony, complete with fancily printed programs. Mrs. L. Bradford Prince, wife of the former territorial governor, was shepherdess of the affair.

Working through the local chapter of the Daughters of the American Revolution, she raised the needed $50 and ordered the stone from the Cemetery Monument Works in Denver. It was intended to grace the plaza forever, as a constant reminder of the glory and hardships associated with the Santa Fe Trail.

Occupying second place in my affections is the Beginning-of-the-Trail Monument at the little hamlet of New Franklin, in central Missouri. The place styles itself "Cradle of the Santa Fe Trail," for it was from near there that William Becknell in 1821 launched the first successful crossing of the prairies to New Mexico and in the bargain wrote himself into the history books.

To the Franklin monument is affixed a large brass plaque with raised letters and a picture of Becknell's mule train in relief. The inscription is far more dramatic than the simple one in Santa Fe. It reads: "This trail, one of the great highways of the world stretched nearly one thousand miles, from Missouri to New Mexico, from civilization to sundown."

There in Franklin, on my first visit, I looked westward past green-robed bluffs to the bottomlands leading down to the banks of the mighty Missouri River. And gazing across the dark waters, I imagined that I could see, in sequence, the many trail landmarks studding the route all the way to Santa

Fe. Their colorful names, as familiar to me as to the wagon-masters, conjured up images of shouting teamsters, rumbling wagon wheels, and rattling trace chains.

Follow the Santa Fe Trail today and you will still find them, places like Arrow Rock, Malta Bend, Fort Osage, Cave Spring, New Santa Fe (a village on the Missouri–Kansas border), The Narrows, 110 Mile Creek, Council Grove, Lost Spring, Turkey Creek, Buffalo Bill's Well, Plum Buttes, Fort Zarah, Pawnee Rock, Cimarron Crossing, La Jornada, Willow Bar, The Rabbit Ears, Point of Rocks, Rock Crossing of the Canadian, Wagon Mound, La Junta, San Miguel del Vado, Pecos Pueblo, Glorieta Pass, Rock Corral, and at last, the foot of the rainbow itself, the plaza at Santa Fe. The majesty of history resides in those place names.

In fact more people than ever are retracing the old trail these days, as enthusiasm for its story grows. In 1987 it became a National Historic Trail under the jurisdiction of the National Park Service, an elevation in status that proved highly newsworthy. A series of recent historic-preservation projects along this pioneer route have also attracted attention. A national organization, the Santa Fe Trail Association, was formed in 1986 and in a short time has taken the lead in commemorative and historical endeavors. Finally authors and scholars have been led to examine neglected facets of the trail's story and to publish new books, offering fresh insights and arousing still more interest in the subject.

In this book I have assembled a collection of my trail pieces that appeared originally in a wide assortment of periodicals and thus, for the most part, are no longer easily accessible. In part I can be found a three-chapter overview of trail history. Part II contains a half dozen scholarly items that add new data to our general fund of information. And in part III I present a number of vignettes—thumbnail sketches of people, places, and events associated with the Santa Fe Trail. An acknowledgment section at the end furnishes the publication references, indicating where the collected pieces first appeared.

Learning about the Santa Fe Trail can be an adventure filled with exciting discovery. It is my hope that this book might contribute something to the building and enrichment of that experience.

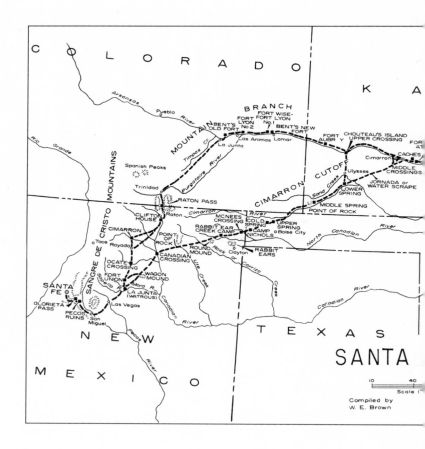

SOURCES:
Joseph C. Brown Map, 1827; Josiah Gregg Map, 1844; Lt. John G. Parke Map, 1851; Kansas State Historical Society Map, 1913; Kenyon Riddle Map, 1949; S.C.S. Aerial Photographs; U.S. G.S. – Army Map Service Maps; Field Work, 1958, 1962.

PART ONE

THE OLD
TRAIL TO SANTA FE

I

TRAILING SOUTHWEST

A Beginning

AMONG THE HISTORIC pathways to the Great West, perhaps none was filled with more romance and adventure than the trail that ran southwest across the plains to Santa Fe. Unlike the emigrant routes to Oregon, California, and Utah, this was a commercial road used mainly by Missouri merchants and freighters who each summer's season took their wagons to the markets of New Mexico and even Chihuahua. When the Santa Fe Trail was opened in 1821, James Monroe was president, and many old soldiers were still living who had fought for independence with General George Washington. When it closed almost sixty years later, the Civil War had been over for a decade and a half, and most of the other famous western trails were long since abandoned.

It was the profit motive, pure and simple, that gave birth to and nourished the overland trade to Santa Fe. In 1821 the new state of Missouri was languishing in the economic doldrums, so that its citizens looked hungrily toward the Mexican provinces, rich in silver coin, beaver pelts, and mules.

At the start business was in the hands of impoverished farmers and small tradesmen, who were in the habit of mortgaging their property to raise the sums needed to enter the New Mexican trade. Rarely could a single individual afford more than a dozen wagons, and the majority had far fewer. All had to sell out quickly and return from Santa Fe by year's end to pay off creditors. Within a few years, however, the amateurs began to fade from the scene, especially as the volume and value of the traffic increased. They were replaced by sturdy, well-capitalized mercantile firms in towns like Lexington, Independence, and Westport, which sent out annual caravans bearing goods for the Mexican trade worth hundreds of thousands of dollars.

Yet there was something beyond profit that in time drew travelers to the Santa Fe Trail. It seems an added attraction was to be found in the entire experience itself—the forming up of a caravan on the Missouri border, the unwinding journey across the sunlit plains, the excitement of a buffalo hunt or even an Indian attack that quickened the blood, and at last the arrival at the foot of the trail in a foreign land.

Josiah Gregg, chief chronicler of the Santa Fe trade, claimed that his comings and goings on the trail developed in him a passion for prairie life that he thought he would never survive. Years later an aging teamster elaborated upon that theme for a reporter from the *Kansas City Star*. "There was something about the plains that used to drag us out upon the trails," he reflected wistfully.

In the spring when the wild plums blossomed and perfumed the air, and the bluestem waved and the buffalo grass began to get velvety, the call was mighty strong. It was like the sea luring the sailor. And I've never had such pleasant days since, nor such hard ones either. Some way there was music in the chucking wheels of a wagon carrying sixty-five or seventy hundred weight and rattling across the plains. And there was the spice of adventure in it all. Not much pay though— $16 to $35 a month.[1]

At least part of the trail's appeal lay in the magic associated with the city of Santa Fe. Until Mexico won independence in 1821, it had been a remote outpost of Spain's empire, a bastion protecting Chihuahua's silver mines to the south and closed to outsiders. Lieutenant Zebulon Pike, brought there as a prisoner in 1806 after his small exploring party strayed beyond the limits of the Louisiana Purchase, was among the first Americans to get a view beyond the guarded veil. The book of his experiences, published after his return home, excited the interest of fellow countrymen and initially alerted them to the commercial possibilities residing in the Mexican territories. It also helped cast a bright glow over the name Santa Fe, endowing it with mystery and romance.

In the early years, the Missourians entering the Mexican trade were narrow in outlook and experience, having for the most part never ventured outside the boundaries of their own nation. Therefore Santa Fe, located as it was in another country, with different language and customs, appeared to them exotic beyond description. Its very strangeness exerted a magnetic pull.

The commercial center of St. Louis attracted merchants, both American and Mexican, involved in the Santa Fe trade. (after Pancoast)

Added to that, of course, were the attractive financial rewards to be reaped in the old Spanish city. Santa Fe's plaza not only marked the end of the trail from Missouri but the beginning of the Chihuahua Trail that pointed toward richer markets beyond. Merchants from northern Mexico met Yankee traders in Santa Fe, bought from them at wholesale, and freighted the wares down to their own stores. Thereby New Mexico's capital was transformed into a flourishing commercial center, a status it had never enjoyed under Spain.

From the vantage point of the American frontier, all this meant that Santa Fe sparkled lustrously, like a pot of gold at rainbow's end. It became a place to go to find wealth and adventure. The final verse in a contemporary song summed up the matter handily:

Then, hold your horses, Billy,
Just hold them for a day;
I've crossed the River Jordan
And I'm bound for Santa Fe. [2]

Unfortunately, as so often happens with romantic myths, the encounter with reality brought a letdown. The narrow dirt streets of the city, the flat-roofed buildings of unfired adobe brick, and the unattractive habits of the residents left most American newcomers sorely disappointed. Still an abiding picturesqueness determined that Santa Fe never quite lost its reputation as a Mecca for the eagerly curious and the adventure-minded.

A rather undistinguished, if enterprising, individual from Franklin, Missouri, William Becknell by name, was the man who started it all. In the summer of 1821, rumors of Mexican independence reached Franklin, a river town in the central part of the state and at that moment the farthest settlement west of St. Louis. Becknell, whose economic fortunes were at a low ebb, decided on a bold gamble. Placing an advertisement in the *Missouri Intelligencer,* he issued a call for men to accompany him on a trading expedition to the Comanches. That seems to have been a ploy to disguise his real destination, Santa Fe. In any event a handful of daring souls responded, and by early September they were on the trail leading a pack string of mules.

Becknell struck west across Kansas to the Great Bend of the Arkansas River, then followed its course upstream into present Colorado. Crossing to the south bank and into Mexican territory somewhere in the vicinity of the future site of Bent's Fort, he angled down to Raton Pass, a high and rocky breach in the mountains that gave access to the New Mexico plains beyond. By November 16 the traders were in Santa Fe, pleased to discover Mexican independence a reality and, with it, a new policy of open commerce. Disposing of his merchandise quickly, Becknell was back in Franklin by January. When he displayed his hoard of silver pesos, he was the envy of his neighbors.

Not one to rest on laurels, Becknell made plans at once to pay Santa Fe another visit. But now he decided to try the journey with freight wagons, which were able to carry many times the weight and bulk of a mule string. So in May he set forth with three wagons, the first ever to cross the plains. He followed his route of the year before as far as western Kansas, but there he turned aside and pioneered a new road, one that was not only shorter but avoided the treacherous climb over Raton Pass.

Near the Dodge City of a later day, he forded the Arkansas and plunged southwest fifty miles across an arid wasteland that would soon become infamous as the Jornada, a term in Spanish that meant a "desert march." (Americans, unused to foreign sounds, pronounced it "Horn Alley.") At the far side, he and his thirsty stock reached the Cimarron River, here only a dry bed, but water could be found by digging a shallow well in the sand. Ascending the Cimarron through the Oklahoma Panhandle, he was brought at last to the Wagon Mound, noted trail landmark in New Mexico. A few days later he was again on the Santa Fe plaza. He had

The packet *John D. Perry* was typical of the steamboats that carried freight and passengers up the Missouri River to landings at the head of the Santa Fe Trail. (author's collection)

proved that wagon travel over the plains was practical . . . and profitable.

William Becknell scarcely had an inkling of what his efforts would produce in the years to come. Nor did he perceive that by taking wagons to Santa Fe, he was walking straight into history. Long after his death (in 1856), the great historian of the American fur trade, Hiram M. Chittenden, would bestow upon him the title "Father of the Santa Fe Trail," an accolade that seems his without question.[3]

So exactly how did the overland trade develop in the period after Becknell's inaugural venture? And what was its precise contribution to the expansion of the American frontier? The answers are to be found in the first twenty-five years of the trail's history, during what might be termed its golden age. It was that span of a quarter century that produced the best-known and most widely read accounts by travelers such as Josiah Gregg, Matt Field, Albert Pike, Alphonso Wetmore, and, toward the last, Susan Magoffin. From the pages of their writings come many of the images that have shaped our notion of what it was like to accompany a freight caravan over the boundless plains to Santa Fe, in the days of the Mexican Republic.

The growth of commerce and traffic proceeded in an orderly manner, almost by carefully defined stages. The decade of the 1820s, which witnessed the birth of the trade, was a time of discovery and experimentation, when the Yankee merchants struggled to work out the new business patterns and freighting techniques required in their dealings with Mexico. In the same period, the federal government snapped to attention when Missouri's powerful Senator Thomas Hart Benton demanded that Congress lend support to the suddenly flourishing commerce on the western border.

Money was appropriated in response to survey the trail and to purchase a right-of-way from tribes along the route, guaranteeing safe passage of the caravans. In 1825 the surveyor Joseph Brown was set upon the task. He was accompanied by Indian commissioners under the leadership of George Sibley, the former government factor, or trader, at Fort Osage. Sibley and his associates negotiated a treaty with the Osage at the crossing of the Neosho River, a place known thereafter as Council Grove. Another treaty was successfully concluded with the Kansas Indians farther west. But the most dangerous tribes—Pawnee, Cheyenne, Comanche, and

Major George C. Sibley, chief figure in the government survey party of 1825. (author's collection)

Kiowa—could not be reached. Brown carried out his survey in a professional manner. Yet neither it nor the rather casual Indian treaties had any lasting impact on the trail's story. The episode, however, did signal that Washington had become aware of the importance of the infant trade with Santa Fe. That awareness was transformed into action in 1829, when growing hostility by the Plains Indians prompted the federal authorities to provide an escort of infantry to accompany the New Mexico–bound traders as far as the international boundary on the Arkansas.

In the meanwhile the head of the Santa Fe Trail had shifted from little Franklin to the new community of Independence, situated one hundred miles farther west and near the Kansas border. Established in 1827, Independence was favorably placed on high, wooded ground, four miles south of its landing on the Missouri River. It was also blessed with fine pastureland closeby and what one contemporary newspaper called "excellent never failing spring water."4 Those natural advantages were quickly grasped by persons of vision, who foresaw the day when the town would boom as a merchandising and trail center. One of them was James Aull, member of a prominent mercantile family from Lexington. He established the first store in Independence by late 1827, with Samuel C. Owens as manager. Both men became heavily involved in commerce with the Mexican provinces.

Within five years Independence came to dominate the Santa Fe trade as an outfitting point. The 1830s were the decade of consolidation, when businessmen and freighters in growing numbers congregated there, assembled crates and

Courthouse Square in Independence, Missouri, when it was the "Queen City of Western Trails." (author's collection)

bales of goods brought upriver by steamboat from St. Louis, and formed their mighty caravans of prairie schooners. That activity inevitably attracted a host of backup craftsmen, such as blacksmiths, farriers, wagon makers and wheelwrights, gunsmiths, saddlers, and harness makers. Neighboring farmers also profited through the sale of agricultural products and livestock to outfitters.

By the early 1830s the customs associated with the forming up of a wagon train had clearly taken shape. The average merchant, as independent as a wild jackass, was loath to submit to the rules of a large caravan, except when danger absolutely compelled it. But the increased threat of Indian troubles forced them to join in convoys for protection. Still they held off to the last possible moment, each trader departing Independence on his own with drovers and wagons.

The old Kaw Indian Mission, Council Grove. It was here beside the Neosho River in eastern Kansas that final organization of the caravans took place. (author's photo)

Council Grove, 150 miles into eastern Kansas, was the accepted rendezvous. To that point the country was safe, but beyond, hostilities with the Indians could be expected at any time.

Two significant tasks were performed at the Council Grove. Since the last large stand of hardwoods to be found on the Santa Fe Trail grew here, the men felled trees and fashioned spare axles and wagon tongues, which were lashed beneath the bodies of the schooners, ready for use in an emergency. The second chore was the organization of the caravan and election of officers. Often there was fierce rivalry

Lost Spring, Kansas, on the open prairie west of Council Grove, was a popular overnight stop for Santa Fe–bound caravans. (author's photo)

and electioneering for the positions of captain, lieutenants, pilot (that is, scout), and commander of the guards. On occasion the bitterness engendered by the campaign would surface in a moment of crises far down the trail.

By this period the route west of Council Grove had become a well-scored trace in the rolling prairie. The way led past the familiar campsites at Diamond Spring and Lost Spring to the crossings of the Little Arkansas and Cow Creek, thence by Plum Buttes to Pawnee Rock, just beyond the Arkansas's Great Bend. Pawnee Rock gained renown in trail annals as an autograph register where travelers paused and carved their names, while keeping an eye peeled for lurking Comanches and Kiowas. Later in the century, when the rock was heavily quarried, most of the historic signatures were lost.

From there the Santa Fe Trail slanted southwestward, keeping the Arkansas River in sight on the left. Upstream from the later-day Dodge City, the route split, forming the two principal branches of the trail, as they had been delineated by Becknell in 1821 and 1822. The longer, righthand fork continued to follow the valley of the Arkansas as far as Bent's Fort, the massive adobe fur-trading post built by Charles and William Bent and Cerán St. Vrain in 1833. That place became a joyous recreation stop on the road to Santa Fe, since it boasted a billiard parlor and barroom and offered weary overlanders a good night's rest free from the worry of Indian attack. What most of them recalled afterward were the resplendent peacocks that wandered the compound freely, together with a pet beaver. When the beaver tumbled into an open barrel of molasses and perished, he was universally mourned.

This longer road via Colorado and Raton Pass was called the Mountain Branch, or sometimes the Bent's Fort Cutoff of the Santa Fe Trail. The shorter route was the one that forded the Arkansas in western Kansas, traversed the dreaded Jornada to the valley of the Cimarron, and followed it to New Mexico, passing the memorable landmarks at Wagon Bed Spring (where Jedediah Smith was slain by Comanches in 1831), Point of Rocks, Willow Bar, Cold Spring, and the Rabbit Ears. That fork was referred to as either the Desert Branch or the Cimarron Cutoff. The two divisions united

This body of a Santa Fe style freight wagon is on display at Bent's Old Fort, Colorado. (author's photo)

again at La Junta, about twenty miles east of Las Vegas (The Meadows), which was the first settlement in New Mexico. The final leg of the trail made its way through the quaint villages of Tecolote, San Miguel del Vado, and Pecos, reaching at last the dusty plaza in Santa Fe.

Josiah Gregg, who made the first of five trips over the nine-hundred-mile length of trail in 1831, became thoroughly familiar with all the popular campsites and featured landmarks between Independence and Santa Fe. He described them in unvarnished, factual detail in his classic work *Commerce of the Prairies* (1844), a volume that was regarded as the basic handbook for those following in his wagon tracks. It remains today a prime source of firsthand information on the subject.

By the advent of the 1840s, Gregg had retired from the trade and the course of events was turning in unexpected directions. The new decade ushered in an era of change and crises, one that would bring a transformation in the character of traffic on the Santa Fe Trail. Signs of change were first visible on Courthouse Square in Independence.

For one thing dapper Mexican merchants in flashy clothes and large hats, waited upon by roughly dressed drovers and servants, had suddenly become a common spectacle on the square. These men from Santa Fe or Albuquerque or from the silver mining cities of Chihuahua had caught the excitement that fast profits always breed. Why not cash in on this extraordinary business, they reasoned, and not leave it all to the Americans. So drawing upon native wits and nerve, they formed their own ox trains and traveling the Santa Fe Trail in reverse, as it were, they betook themselves to *Los Estados* ("The States") to buy at wholesale. Returning home they enjoyed an advantage in the marketplace because the Mexican government charged its own citizens less in import duties than it did foreigners. Thus the Mexican traders could easily undersell their American competitors. In that manner the foundation was laid for the development of a number of princely fortunes.

Astonishing to tell, by the year 1843 Mexicans had gained the edge and had become the majority among travelers moving over the trail. They had their own distinctive ways of

The original wagon box that carried the gold and silver of Antonio José Chávez, 1843, when he was held up and murdered in eastern Kansas. (author's photo)

handling stock, moving freight, and supervising drovers through a *mayordomo,* or wagonmaster. But largely owing to the scarcity of records, their substantial participation in the overland adventure has passed virtually unnoticed.

An exception was Antonio José, Chávez, trader and owner of an hacienda in the Rio Grande Valley. Gregg and other writers of the time took note of him because of his tragic fate. Coming from Santa Fe in April of 1843 with a small party and a chest full of silver to make his purchases, Don Antonio was captured by American "land pirates" near the Little Arkansas crossing and brutally murdered. The crime threw the Missouri frontier into an uproar, since it threatened to disrupt relations with Mexico and hinder commerce of the trail. Consequently a posse was assembled in Independence and sent to the prairies, and dragoons were dispatched from Fort Leavenworth. Eventually the search produced the culprits, and the two guilty of the actual killing were tried and hanged the following year in St. Louis.

Another event of 1843 was destined to alter further the face of activity on Independence Square. That was the beginning of the great Oregon migration. The town, poised as it was on the outer line of settlement and fully able to supply the needs of wagon pioneers, stood ready to capitalize on the new opportunity for business. In 1844 municipal fathers placed the value of the Santa Fe trade at $500,000, while services and goods provided to the inrush of Oregon emigrants was estimated at $50,000.[5] Francis Parkman, who took to the Oregon Trail in 1846, speaks of the color and excitement that enveloped Independence during those days of what he called "the great western movement." Even with the vivid description that he and others furnish, it is difficult to conjure up an authentic sense of the enthusiasm and air of expectation animating the people who congregated on Courthouse Square, ready to take their leave for the glowing Southwest or Northwest. In the twentieth century, Independence remembering that heady time in her own past would crown herself "Queen City of the Trails."

But even as Parkman wrote, an eclipse was beginning to cast a shadow upon Independence's hard-won prosperity. A

Exuberant teamsters approaching Santa Fe at the end of the trail. (after Gregg)

rival named Westport was in the wings, eager to usurp the title of trailhead. Eight miles upriver from Independence, paddle wheelers were finding an easy berth at Westport Landing, the future Kansas City. The new town of Westport, four miles south of the landing, could offer plenty of spring water and open pasture to wagoners preparing to embark for the Far West. And gradually as more mercantile houses opened their doors, it was able to supply the full range of provisions and equipment needed by trail parties. By the mid-1840s, local merchant William R. Bernard could write: "The prairies south of the town . . . were covered with tents and wagons and appeared like the camp of a great army."[6] From that point forward, Westport's ascendancy would be achieved at the expense of Independence.

The Santa Fe trade, however, experienced an abrupt jolt in 1846, with the outbreak of the Mexican War. In late spring President James K. Polk ordered Colonel (soon to be General) Stephen W. Kearny to muster regular troops and volunteers at Fort Leavenworth and invade New Mexico. Kearny elected to follow the Mountain Branch of the Santa Fe Trail and to use Bent's Fort as a staging ground for his conquest. He sent a troop riding well in advance of the main army with orders to stop caravans that were already on their way to New Mexico. He wanted none of the supplies they were carrying to fall into enemy hands. Nevertheless one trader, Albert Speyer, who was running fine Mississippi rifles to Mexico, slipped through and delivered his cargo. In the end it made little difference. Kearny's soldiers, fresh off the trail, marched unopposed into the Santa Fe plaza on August 18, 1846. When they lowered the Mexican tricolor and raised in its place the stars and bars over the old Spanish Governors' Palace, it signaled a new day for New Mexico and for overland commerce as well.

Now all at once, both ends of the Santa Fe Trail were in American hands. Down came the foreign customs house and inspections that had been part of the trade under Mexican rule. That was the most immediate and noticeable effect. But other changes were soon in the offing, with the result that life and business on the Santa Fe Trail began to undergo a profound transformation. However, that is a story that belongs to the second half of the trail's history.

NOTES

1. *Kansas City Star,* January 9, 1911.

2. W. W. H. Davis, *El Gringo, or New Mexico & Her People* (New York: Harper & Brothers, 1857), 4.

3. Current residents of Clarksville, Texas, near which William Becknell settled after his Santa Fe Trail experience, say that his family always pronounced "Becknell" with the accent on the first syllable.

4. *Missouri Intelligencer,* June 27, 1827.

5. Eugene T. Wells, "The Growth of Independence, Missouri, 1827–1850," *Bulletin of the Missouri Historical Society* 16 (October 1959): 41.

6. William R. Bernard, "Westport and the Santa Fe Trade," *Transactions of the Kansas State Historical Society* 9 (1906): 556.

2

A NEW DAY
After 1848

B‍Y THE T‍REATY of Guadalupe Hidalgo, ending the Mexican War in 1848, the provinces of New Mexico and California, with everything in between, were formally ceded to the United States. With that the story of the Santa Fe Trail entered its second phase. Some of the initial sparkle was lost, now that the foot of the trail was under American rather than Mexican control. However, the international aspect of the overland trade, which had lent such color and excitement to its early years, did not completely disappear.

A significant number of Missouri merchants continued on with their caravans to the new boundary at El Paso and proceeded to Chihuahua City to dispose of their freight. William McCoy of Independence, writing to his bride-to-be in the spring of 1848, declared that Mexican mania had seized residents of the town and added that "almost everyone in coming to this country [that is, Missouri] becomes infected and rests uneasy until he has completed the great achievement of going to Mexico."[1] At the moment he wrote, the trail from

Santa Fe in the 1870s. The street in the center leading toward the plaza is the tag end of the Santa Fe Trail. (Museum of New Mexico, negative no. 10205)

Independence to Council Grove was reported to be one continuous encampment of Santa Fe and Chihuahua traders.

The commotion on the Missouri border ascended to an even higher level the following year, 1849, when news of the discovery at Sutter's Mill brought in a flood of gold seekers, eager to outfit and depart for the new Promised Land of California. The majority of the forty-niners chose to follow the central route that began with the Oregon Trail. But a fair number elected to go by way of Santa Fe, shorter in miles but considered to be more dangerous.

Young Edwin Bryant, leaving for the goldfields, encountered just beyond the Lone Elm campground, near the eastern border of Kansas, a worn and weather-battered caravan arriving from Mexico. Bryant interviewed the grizzled wagonmaster, a man well-versed in western trails. "He said that the journey to Santa Fe and Chihuahua was one of great fatigue and hardship, but that the journey to California was infinitely more so; that our lives would be shortened ten years by the trip, and before we returned, our heads would be white, not with the frosts of age, but from the effects of exposure and extreme hardships."[2]

Perils and privations had been part of the trail experience since Becknell's pioneering journey in 1821. Nevertheless, in the period after the Mexican War even more problems beset overlanders. That proved to be something of a surprise to knowledgeable observers of the day, who had assumed that the Santa Fe trade had reached maturity and serious obstacles to travel were receding into the past. William McCoy, in the letter to his lady, gave voice to that view when he told her that the Santa Fe Trail had become "a beaten highway the whole distance & so much travelled, that it is a tame affair."[3] In that he was very much mistaken.

A sudden flare-up of Indian troubles was the first thing to cause concern. Before 1846 trail traffic had experienced only sporadic and small-scale attacks. But with the march of General Kearny's Army of the West over the Mountain Branch, soon followed by soldier units on their way to garrison duty in New Mexico, the Plains tribes took alarm. With the sudden increase in both military and civilian caravans, they also perceived new opportunities for plunder, and raids multiplied accordingly.

To meet the threat, the War Department called up five companies of Missouri volunteers and formed an Indian bat-

A scene familiar to travelers on the Santa Fe Trail. (after O. O. Howard)

talion under Lieutenant Colonel William Gilpin (later governor of the Colorado Territory). Making a quick assessment, Gilpin found to his dismay that recent losses on the trail amounted to 47 men killed, 330 wagons burned, and 6,500 head of stock stolen.[4] The figures suggested a need for quick action.

The Indian Batallion patrolled the trail as far as the first New Mexican settlements and also furnished escorts for caravans moving in both directions. It fought a handful of small engagements with war parties and in July 1848 assaulted a Comanche camp in southwestern Kansas containing six hundred warriors. These actions were intended to overawe the Indians and force them to leave wagon trains in peace. And

William Gilpin, commander of the Indian Battalion. (author's collection)

the show of strength did provide some temporary relief. But when the battalion's term of enlistment was up at the end of one year, the job was far from complete. Based on his first-hand experience, Colonel Gilpin recommended that the army build a series of forts along the trail, as the only sure way to guarantee the safety of travelers.

Shortly thereafter the soundness of his proposal was underscored in grim fashion by two bloody incidents that occurred on the western end of the Cimarron Cutoff. In the fall of 1849, Independence merchant James M. White was attacked by Apaches at New Mexico's Point of Rocks. He and his teamsters were killed and his wife and small daughter carried away. A military search party, with Kit Carson as one of the guides, pursued the raiders. But when the camp was overtaken, the Apaches fled, leaving behind the still-warm body of Mrs. White.

The next spring Apaches and Utes waylaid a mail party of ten men from Fort Leavenworth at the foot of the Wagon Mound. The members of the party, all heavily armed, put up a furious defense before being overwhelmed. A week later a relief column came upon the scene and discovered the victims' bones scattered by the wolves and the U.S. mail strewn upon the sandy plain.

Both tragedies received wide coverage in the eastern press and spurred the War Department to begin construction of forts on the Santa Fe Trail. Among the first and the largest was Fort Union (1851), placed near the strategic junction of the Cimarron Cutoff and the Mountain Branch, about twenty miles east of Las Vegas. In the same year, Fort Atkin-

Point of Rocks, New Mexico. Near here the James M. White party was massacred in 1849. (after Dewitt Peters)

son (called by the troops Fort Sodom) was built near the crossing of the Arkansas, just west of present Dodge City. Other posts followed in succession over the next two decades: Fort Larned (1859) in central Kansas, Fort Wise (1860; renamed Fort Lyon) in southeastern Colorado, Fort Zarah (1864) at the Great Bend of the Arkansas, and Forts Dodge and Aubry (1865), both on the Arkansas in western Kansas. All played a vital role in keeping the lane open between Missouri and New Mexico, and some of the liveliest chronicles of the trail were handed down by officers and enlisted men who almost daily faced arrows and the scalping knife.

A Santa Fe caravan crossing the Great Plains. (after Twitchell)

Another problem that became more acute after the Mexican War was disease. In the early years, typhoid, chronic dysentery, and especially malaria were the scourges of the trail. The last had been treated by bleeding until 1832, when Dr. John Sappington of Arrow Rock, Missouri, began manufacturing quinine Anti-Fever Pills. Thereafter every overlander with sense tucked a little box of Sappington's pills in his kit.

The most devastating malady, however, was Asiatic cholera, which struck the trail with full force in 1849. Introduced by way of the port of New Orleans, it traveled up the Mississippi to St. Louis, where four thousand people, including seventeen physicians died. Steamboat passengers on the Missouri carried it to the head of the Santa Fe Trail, and soon graves dotted the route to Council Grove and beyond. Merchants, teamsters, forty-niners, soldiers, and Indians all succumbed. It was reported that half the Cheyenne tribe perished in the epidemic.

From that time on, cholera remained endemic on the trail. One member of a freight caravan leaving Leavenworth for New Mexico in 1852 wrote that the wagons passed through clouds of acrid black smoke emitted by barrels of burning tar placed on every street corner. Once on the plains, the wagons themselves were fumigated with smudge pots. The cause of the disease was then unknown, but a common theory held that it was spread through the air, which could be sanitized by smoke. Other theories held that it was caused by too frequent bathing, eating rancid cucumbers, and sin. Remedies for cholera were no more scientific—dosing with bitters or using antibilious powders. New Mexican traders preferred a "medicine" of Penguin whiskey (a popular brand exported to Santa Fe), heavily laced with their own ground red chile. Not until 1883, three years after the trail closed, was it discovered that cholera was a water-borne disease.

But neither Indian raids nor cholera discouraged travel to Santa Fe after midcentury. Indeed with the growth of military freighting, needed to supply the new garrisons on the trail and those beyond in the far Southwest, and the expansion of commercial freighting, the volume of traffic mounted year by year. Contributing to this increase was the appearance of regular stagecoach service, a convenience that had been lacking during the previous period.

The first stage set out from Independence Square in the summer of 1850. The firm of Waldo, Hall & Company owned the line, which received a government contract to carry the U.S. mail to New Mexico. The senior partner, David Waldo, was a physician long involved in the Santa Fe trade, who also acted as a contractor for government freight on the Oregon Trail. According to press accounts, the company's coaches were "got up in splendid style, and are each capable of conveying eight passengers. The bodies are beautifully painted, and made water-tight, with a view of using them as boats in ferrying streams. The team consists of six mules."[5]

Initially a one-way fare to Santa Fe was $200. From Independence the stages required just over seven weeks for a round-trip. Until 1861 the shorter Cimarron Cutoff was used, but with outbreak of the Civil War in that year and the threat of interference from Texan Confederates, the route was shifted to the Mountain Branch. For the first ten years or so, there were no relay stations beyond Council Grove. Therefore the coach was accompanied by a wagon carrying provisions and a full camping outfit. At night passengers cooked their own meals trailside and spread blankets upon the ground. In 1860 service, which had already gone to twice-monthly, was increased to weekly and stations were established every twelve to twenty miles. These stations offered changes of mules, allowing the stages to travel at night and cutting the time to Santa Fe in half. Soon after the Civil War, daily service was inaugurated.

Perhaps because of the romantic picture of stagecoach travel presented by Hollywood's western films, it is often as-

Sutler's Store at Fort Dodge, Kansas, on the Santa Fe Trail. (from *Harper's Weekly,* May 25, 1867)

sumed that a trip over the Santa Fe Trail in one of those old conveyances was an adventurous lark. In fact it was an ordeal that few who lived through the experience desired to repeat. The food was of the roughest sort, usually rock hard biscuits, sour beans, and bitter coffee. Not until the 1870s did a few stations furnish meals that invited favorable comment, among them Kozlowski's Ranch on the Pecos, where the proprietor's wife prepared fresh trout, and the Clifton House Station south of Raton Pass, a hostelry with what approached gourmet cooking.

A reenactment soldier poses at the entrance of the parade ground, Fort Union, New Mexico, near the junction of the Cimarron Cutoff and the Mountain Branch. (author's photo)

Worse than the table fare, however, was the sheer discomfort. Seating in the coaches was cramped, the jolting interminable, and rest stops few and brief. When the weather turned cold, passengers shivered under buffalo robes. Most unpleasant of all was the inevitable bout of motion sickness caused by the constant rocking of the stage. George Courtright, who made the trip in 1864, said: "About the second day what is known as coach fever comes on accompanied with an excruciating headache, and every jolt of the coach is almost unbearable."[6] Several years later, tourist J. H. Beadle, who was similarly afflicted with coach fever, described his condition upon alighting in the Santa Fe plaza: "There was a horrible feeling about my stomach, as if millions of insects were crawling from there up to my head; and a sensation of pitching forward and backward, feeling as if my head was unscrewed, loose, and liable at any moment to be jerked off."[7]

All of this was compounded by the physical danger inherent in every run over the trail. Swollen rivers sometimes had to be forded. On the Mountain Branch the perilous climb to the summit of Raton Pass could prove nerve-shattering, particularly, as happened on at least two occasions, when the stage turned over. Then until the middle 1870s, the specter of attack by Indians was ever present. Since the warriors had no use for a captured coach, they customarily burned it. But once in western Kansas, they tried to drag a stage away by tieing it to their horses' tails. Unfortunately for the poor beasts, their tails were pulled off and left with the stranded vehicle.

In looking for other changes that overtook the Santa Fe Trail in its later years, one soon notices a rise in the number and classes of women travelers. Prior to 1846 a few native New Mexican ladies made the trip east, but even fewer American women went to Santa Fe. Susan Magoffin, riding the merchant train in the wake of Kearny's conquering army, actually claimed she was the first, although that was not so. But the situation quickly changed once the Southwest belonged to the United States.

That is not to say that women ever became numerous on the Santa Fe route. The stock image of the pioneer wife in her slat-sided sunbonnet marching beside her husband and an ox-drawn covered wagon, while appropriate for the Oregon and Mormon emigrant trails, hardly fits the picture of the Santa Fe road. Still there were *some* women, memorable because of their rarity, but also because a few of them wrote valuable journals or reminiscences.

Among the vanguard were female relations of merchants, of government officials newly appointed to the New Mexico Territory, and of officers posted to the forts springing up along the trail. A few wives and daughters of Protestant missionaries braved a crossing of the prairies as well. Worth special note are several contingents of Sisters of Loretto and Sisters of Charity, conducted to Santa Fe by Bishop John B. Lamy.

In 1867 the bishop was returning to New Mexico with a party of nuns and priests he had recruited in the East. The Indian danger was at its peak, and for safety he joined a large caravan of New Mexicans heading home from a season's trading in Missouri. West of Fort Dodge the train was encircled by a howling horde of several hundred Comanches and Kiowas. Lamy climbed upon a wagon wheel, exposing his person to a hail of bullets and arrows, and directed the defense.

Eventually the attack was beaten off. But unhappily the youngest nun, eighteen-year-old Sister Mary Alphonsa Thompson, had been stricken with such terror that it is said she died of fright. A hasty service was arranged, and she was buried in a solitary grave on the arid plain.

Probably the largest single category of women to be found on the trail was composed of those who went with their men-

The parade ground and restored buildings at Fort Larned, Kansas. (author's photo)

folk in the rush to the Colorado goldfields in 1859. Many of these so-called Pike's Peakers followed the Smoky Hill Trail across northern Kansas. But a significant number chose to go by way of the Santa Fe Trail, at least as far as Bent's old fort (which had been abandoned in 1849), where they angled off toward the diggings. One eastbound traveler at the height of the rush observed almost two hundred women among the wagons headed for Colorado.

Julia Archibald Holmes was a member of that small army of ladies. She and her husband joined a company of gold seekers in Lawrence, Kansas, and picked up the Santa Fe road near Council Grove. What lends color to her story is that

Watercolor of San José del Vado, New Mexico, 1869, located at a major trail crossing of the Pecos River. (photo courtesy of Robert R. White)

she was, so far as we know, the first woman to travel the trail wearing reform dress, popularly known as "the bloomer," a costume favored by early-day advocates of women's rights. When Mrs. Holmes asked for permission to do guard duty, the wagonmaster, a courtly Virginian, sternly rebuffed her. He declared the train would be disgraced if a woman was allowed to stand guard. In a letter she wrote petulantly, "He [the wagonmaster] believes that woman is an angel, without any sense, needing the legislation of her brothers to keep her in her place."[8]

The one woman who knew the Santa Fe Trail the best and spoke of it most eloquently was Marian Sloan Russell. In 1852 at age seven she left Fort Leavenworth for Santa Fe with her mother and brother, the first of five such journeys. After the last crossing, she married Lieutenant Richard Rus-

Store of a major mercantile and freighting firm on the trail, Otero, Sellar & Co., Hays City, Kansas, 1878. (Museum of New Mexico, negative no. 9431)

sell at Fort Union and lived in quarters next to Colonel Kit Carson. Kit was engaged in protecting caravans between there and Fort Larned. In her memoirs, dictated when she was ninety, Marian exclaimed: "There have been many things in my life that I have striven to forget, but not those trips over the trail. The lure the old trail held for us! Seems that folks who made those trips in covered wagons never forgot them."9

The death knell of the old Santa Fe Trail was sounded in the 1870s by the advancing railroad. As tracks were pushed west across Kansas, the trail was progressively shortened, with freight wagons and stagecoaches for Santa Fe embarking from

Celebrating the arrival of the railroad in Las Vegas, New Mexico, July 4, 1879. (from *Frank Leslie's Illustrated Newspaper,* August 9, 1879)

each new railhead. The Atchison, Topeka and Santa Fe built along the Mountain Branch, preferring that route over the Cimarron Cutoff because of the coal and timber for ties available in the vicinity of Raton Pass.

By early 1879 the AT&SF had surmounted the pass and entered New Mexico. The following Fourth of July, the rails reached Las Vegas, a scant sixty-five miles east of the capital. For the next few months, the Southern Overland Mail Company continued to send its stagecoaches over the last shrunken stretch of trail. But even that limited service ended in February 1880, when the first train finally pulled into Santa Fe. With the railroad now carrying passengers and freight, the need for the trail was finished.

Augustus A. Hayes, Jr., who rode one of the last stages, remained in town long enough to witness the symbolic end of an era. As he phrased it, "The whistle of the locomotive frightens the burro whom it is to supersede." And he added as an afterthought: "The Santa Fe trade had now passed completely out of the realm of the romantic and into that of the commonplace."[10] By that, of course, he meant that the picturesqueness and high drama accompanying the Ox and Mule Age in the far Southwest were destined to disappear in the Machine Age, which was then at hand. Time has proved him right.

NOTES

1. Eugene T. Wells, "The Growth of Independence, Missouri, 1827–1850," *Bulletin of the Missouri Historical Society* 16 (October 1959): 42.

2. Edwin Bryant, *What I Saw in California* (facsimile edition; Minneapolis: Ross and Haines, 1967), p. 34.

3. Wells, "The Growth of Independence," 43.

4. Thomas L. Karnes, *William Gilpin, Western Nationalist* (Austin: University of Texas Press, 1970); and Leo Oliva, *Soldiers on the Santa Fe Trail* (Norman: University of Oklahoma Press, 1967), 84.

5. *The Western Journal* [St. Louis], September 1850.

6. George Courtright, *An Expedition against the Indians in 1864* (Lithopolis, OH: privately printed, n.d.), 2.

7. J. H. Beadle, *The Undeveloped West, or Five Years in the Territories* (Philadelphia: National Publishing Co., 1873), 449.

8. Julia Archibald Holmes, *A Bloomer Girl on Pike's Peak, 1858* (Denver: Denver Public Library, 1949), 21.

9. Mrs. Hal Russell, ed., *Land of Enchantment: Memoirs of Marian Russell along the Santa Fe Trail* (Albuquerque: University of New Mexico Press, 1981), 91.

10. A. A. Hayes, Jr., *New Colorado and the Santa Fe Trail* (New York: Harper & Brothers, 1880), 159; and R. L. Duffus, *The Santa Fe Trail* (New York: Longmans, Green and Co., 1931), 226.

3

THE TRAIL IN MEMORY

W HEN THE SANTA Fe Trail closed in 1880, after an active life of almost sixty years, it marked the end of a stirring chapter in our frontier history. As the oldest and longest surviving of America's trans-Mississippi pathways to the West, the historic trail to Santa Fe had acquired a halo of romance and accumulated a record of adventure rivaling the Oregon Trail. No writer who deals with westward expansion in a serious manner can fail to grant it abundant laurels for its role in that movement.

But the Santa Fe Trail was more than just a pioneer road, more than an artery of commerce to the far Southwest. In time travelers upon its wide, deep tracks spoke and wrote about their experiences as if they were something entirely new and very special. Young Marian Russell, who made five round-trips between Fort Leavenworth and Santa Fe in the 1850s and 1860s, phrased it best when she said, "The trail [became] our point of outlook upon the universe; the blue sky above us . . . bread and meat for our soul. If you have ever followed the old trail over mountains, through forests, felt the sting of cold, the oppression of heat, the drench of rains and the fury of winds in an old covered wagon you will know what I mean."[1]

Some of the same motives that in the 1830s drew a young Melville to the sea also animated, it would appear, many of the Missouri traders who departed for Santa Fe. For the future author of *Moby Dick* had written: "The necessity of doing something for myself, united to a naturally roving disposition, had now conspired within me, to send me to sea as a sailor."[2] It was a similar combination of necessity and spirit of adventure that set men, and later women, loose on the Santa Fe Trail.

The allusion to Melville and the sea here is particularly apt, for many who made the journey to New Mexico wrote of their crossing of the "prairie ocean" in their huge freight wagons termed "prairie schooners." Embarking from one or another of the Missouri towns, they said they were "leaving port." And of course the community of Westport was a main launching point for the "voyage" to Santa Fe. The vocabulary of seafaring was much a part of plains travel. So much so that in the 1850s, several individuals experimented with wind wagons, that is, wagon bodies rigged with sails, which the owners hoped would blow them and their cargos across the ocean of grass to Santa Fe.

In the rush of six decades, the Santa Fe Trail witnessed all the diverse and sundry traffic common to the frontier. Its travelers included explorers, brigades of mountain men, merchants and traders, Mexicans and Indians, soldiers, gold seekers,

The railroad triumphs over the stagecoach, and the Santa Fe Trail passes into history. (Museum of New Mexico, negative no. 14884)

health seekers, tourists, missionaries, and just plain emigrant folk. Much of what happened on the trail in those early years helped shape the character and future development of the southwestern territories. Given all this it is not surprising that the Santa Fe Trail, after it had slipped into the history books, managed to maintain something of a glamorous mystique.

In February 1880, as the first AT&SF engine steamed into New Mexico's capital on shiny new tracks, a local newspaper had gloated in bold headlines: "Santa Fe's Triumph! The Last Link is Forged in the Iron Chain and the Old Santa Fe Trail Passes into Oblivion!"[3] The words were intended as an epitaph for the now dead era of the trail and as a herald for the coming age of progress. And they implied that since the day of the trail was done, its history could just as well be forgotten.

But that's not quite the way it worked out. As the Santa

Fe Trail receded into the past and memory of it dimmed, people began to appear who seemed unwilling to let it go. Among them were members of the Old Plainsmen's Association, a group of aging freighters and bullwhackers from western Missouri who, after the opening of the twentieth century, foregathered annually at the Independence Fair to swap yarns and entertain younger visitors with tales of wagon trains, Indian fights, and buffalo stampedes. A news reporter observed admiringly that some of these old-timers could still "make a 20-foot bullwhip crack sharper than a six-shooter and snip gnats from the rump of the off ox of the front yoke without turning a hair."[4]

The plainsmen were worried that their story and their contribution to the taming of the West might be passed over and lost. So they laid ambitious plans to erect a bronze statue of a bullwhacker in Independence and fund it through the sale of a proposed book that would recount their individual adventures. But unfortunately their collective energy failed them, and neither the book nor the statue ever appeared. Others, however, were ready to take up the cause.

The most ambitious project to commemorate the Santa Fe Trail was soon unveiled by the formidable ladies of the Daughters of the American Revolution. Precisely who should be credited with the initial idea of placing granite markers along the historic route remains a matter of dispute. One source asserts that Mrs. L. Bradford Prince, wife of the former territorial governor of New Mexico, first raised the issue at a DAR congress in Washington in 1899. At that time she is said to have interested Mrs. W. E. Stanley, wife of the

A fine statue of a Santa Fe wagonmaster, with authentic accouterments, at the Ritz-Carlton–Kansas City. (author's photo)

Kansas governor, who carried the proposal back to her home chapter.[5]

On the other hand, the Kansas DAR has always claimed that its own state regent, Fannie Geiger Thompson, first broached the subject of marking the trail through Kansas at a state conference in 1902. When she died the following year, Mrs. Stanley assumed command of the effort and carried it to completion.[6] That issue aside, what is significant is that the Kansas DAR, upon enlisting broad popular support, managed to get a $1,000 appropriation from the legislature in 1905 to purchase the markers. Additional monies were raised from private sources, including $584 collected by schoolchildren, so that the nine markers originally envisioned eventually came to number ninety-six.

The success in Kansas inspired DAR chapters in Colorado, Missouri, and New Mexico to seek and obtain their own appropriations for trail monuments, with the result that between 1906 and 1912 more than 160 were placed beside the fading route. Usually the unveiling of each was attended by elaborate ceremony, and the trail and its history received a good deal of local press coverage. The dedications of a special beginning-of-the-trail marker at Franklin, Missouri, in 1909 and of the end-of-the-trail marker in Santa Fe two years later attracted large crowds.

Perhaps the most exuberant celebration occurred in Council Grove on August 10, 1907, the eighty-second anniversary of Commissioner George Sibley's treaty with the Osage, on this same site, which secured a right-of-way for the Santa Fe Trail. The marker was placed next to the Council Oak, the huge tree alleged to have been the one that shaded the treaty makers (It blew down in 1958). The usual speeches were followed by "a grand historical parade which embraced every phase of trail life from ox wagons, stage coach, pony express, cowboys, hunters, plainsmen, and ending with

PROGRAMME

of

Exercises at Dedication of Marker at End of Santa Fe Trail

In the Plaza at Santa Fe, New Mexico.

AUGUST 21st, 1911.

1. America.

2. Prayer. . . . . . Rev. Jules Deraches.

3. Introduction and Transference of the Monument
   to the Governor, by Mrs. L. Bradford Prince.
   State Regent D. A. R. for New Mexico.

4. Unveiling of the Monument during the Presentation
   to the Governor, by Miss Madeline Mills.

5. Acceptance and Presentation to City of Santa Fe,
   By Hon. W. J. Mills, Governor of New Mexico.

6. Acceptance of Monument for the City,
   By Hon. Arthur Seligman, Mayor of Santa Fe.

7. Reminiscences of the Trail. . . By Hon. Thos. B. Catron.

8. The Santa Fe Trail and Santa Fe, the Athens of the Southwest,
   by Hon. Nestor Montoya.

9. A Short History of the Trail by Hon. L. Bradford Prince,
   President of the Historical Society of New Mexico.

10. Star Spangled Banner.

Program of one of the many dedicatory ceremonies held upon installation of DAR markers. (from New Mexico State Records Center, Santa Fe) modern carriages and automobiles."[7] It is worth noting that a locked history box was entombed in cement under the marker, the key being deposited with the Kansas State Historical Society along with instructions to open the box in the year 2007.

As the DAR program was getting launched in 1906, it benefited from an event then in progress on the Oregon Trail. Seventy-five-year-old Ezra Meeker, who had migrated to Oregon with his family back in 1852, decided to retrace his route by returning east by wagon and ox team. His intent was to publicize the old trail and get it marked. The attention he received in the national news helped spark interest in pioneer trails generally.

The work of the DAR itself furnished inspiration for the founding of the National Old Trails Road Association at Kansas City in 1912. The purpose of the new group was to push through Congress legislation for the creation of a federal highway system, beginning with a coast-to-coast highway from Baltimore and Washington to Los Angeles. The proposed route was plotted along historic roads and trails of the nineteenth century, with the hope that their precedent might ease passage of a bill and appropriations.

The first federal highway, conceived by George Washington in 1784, was not established by act of Congress until 1806. It initially began at Cumberland, Maryland, and in time was extended across six states to St. Louis. Called the National Road, or sometimes the Cumberland Pike, it became the stellar western route for emigrants on foot, horseback, or in Conestoga wagons. An extension from St. Louis

The nub of the Council Oak's stump, all that remains, can be seen under the roof at left, center. The site is part of the original Council Grove, where wagon trains would organize and elect officers. (author's photo)

westward to Franklin was blazed by Daniel Boone and sur-
veyed by his two sons in 1815. Locally it became known as
the Boone's Lick Road. Then when Congress authorized the
Sibley survey of the path to Santa Fe in 1825, that trail au-
tomatically became part of the federal system.

The whole structure fell apart in 1837, however, when the
government abandoned the concept of maintaining The National Road. The principal reason was that railroads were
entering their spectacular period of growth and, as a result,
other forms of overland travel declined in importance. Not
until the early twentieth century, with the advent of automobiles, was the federal highway concept revived. In the
forefront of its proponents was the Missouri DAR, which
vigorously campaigned to have the projected coast-to-coast
highway follow the Boone's Lick Road and Santa Fe Trail,
both of which they had already marked with handsome granite monuments.

The movement to create the new National Road was side-
tracked by World War I and only got back on course in
1928, when Judge Harry S. Truman of Independence became president of the National Old Trails Association. With
his backing and that of President Calvin Coolidge, the highway bill glided through Congress, and construction of the
first Atlantic and Pacific road soon got under way.

That same year the DAR joined with the association to
sponsor the placing of twelve identical statues of the Pioneer
Mother, called the Madonna of the Trail, in each of the states
through which the new National Road passed. Four of the
ten-foot algonite figures were designated for the Santa Fe

One of the many DAR granite markers along the trail. This one is in Dodge City, Kansas. (author's photo)

Trail, to be located at Lexington, Missouri; Council Grove, Kansas; Lamar, Colorado; and Santa Fe, New Mexico. Because the Santa Fe art colony objected to the conventional style of the sculpture, the Madonna intended for the plaza at the end of the trail was moved south sixty miles to a park in Albuquerque.[8]

The entire marking program of the DAR, stretching across a quarter century, represents an important first chapter in the modern history of the Santa Fe Trail. Not only did it help keep the memory of the trail alive and stimulate public interest in historic preservation, the commemorative efforts also led to some of the first serious research.

As a result of the DAR's work, in which it had closely cooperated, the Kansas State Historical Society in 1912 initiated a project to prepare an accurate and true map of the course of the trail through Kansas. A committee of scholars was appointed to carry out the research in the society's archives in Topeka. In addition elderly wagonmasters and teamsters who had actually driven the trail were interviewed, as were old settlers who remembered where wagon tracks had once been before plowing and weathering erased them. The map, together with explanatory notes, was published by the society in 1913 as part of its *Eighteenth Biennial Report.*

Slowly other serious works dealing with the history of the Santa Fe Trail began to appear. Gregg's *Commerce of the Prairies,* originally published in 1844, had long been the only entire book to deal with the trail story. Then in 1897 Colonel Henry Inman published *The Old Santa Fe Trail,* conceded to be the first formal history of the trail from its opening to its

Colonel Henry Inman wrote the first general history of the trail. (author's collection)

end. Inman had done military service on the trail in the 1860s and had been acquainted with such frontier luminaries as Carson, Custer, and Cody. In 1878 he established a newspaper at Larned on the Pawnee Fork, not far from old Fort Larned. His first hand experience with people and events associated with the trail would seem to qualify him as something of an expert on the subject. But later writers have viewed his book with a jaundiced eye, calling it lively reading but lacking in reliability.

A landmark in trail studies was reached in 1926 when Yale University Press brought out the first edition of Susan Magoffin's diary of 1846–47, under the title *Down the Santa Fe Trail and into Mexico.* This prime document had remained unknown to scholars until Missouri librarian Stella M. Drumm persuaded Magoffin descendants to release it for publication.

The 1930s witnessed a brief flurry of important trail books. At the beginning of the decade, Robert L. Duffus produced *The Santa Fe Trail,* a volume that quickly superseded Inman and became recognized as the standard history of the trail. It was not displaced by Stanley Vestal's *The Old Santa Fe Trail* (1939), which in trying to attract a popular readership faltered in accuracy. Other works of note that appeared in those years included Archer B. Hulbert, ed., *Southwest on the Turquoise Trail: The First Diaries on the Road to Santa Fe* (1930); and James Josiah Webb, *Adventures in the Santa Fe Trade, 1844–1847* (1931). These and similar titles began to provide the solid grounding needed by those who were developing a sincere interest in the authentic history of the trail.

Meanwhile the marking activities of the DAR had come

to a close, and amid the national trauma of the Great Depression and World War II, no other organization stepped forward to promote the Santa Fe Trail. In 1948, however, the American Pioneer Trail Association, through its Kansas City chapter, undertook to mark the entire route between Missouri and New Mexico. Its white oval signs bearing a covered wagon and the words "Santa Fe Trail" have today mostly disappeared, the victims of souvenir hunters.

About 1960 a new group emerged, the Santa Fe Trail Association, spearheaded by New Mexico State Senator William Wheatley. The route was again marked with small metal signs, promotional literature and a guide were issued, and the Rabbit Ears–Clayton Complex was registered as a National Historic Landmark. At the Association's first annual meeting, held in Lyons, Kansas, in 1961, almost three hundred people were in attendance, including the governor of New Mexico and the mayor of Santa Fe. Unfortunately this was also the last annual meeting, because after an auspicious beginning, the organization gradually disintegrated.

While for many years interest in the trail had focused on merely marking it, by the 1950s attention began to shift toward preservation of sites, including wagon ruts and structures. Under the National Historic Landmark Program, launched in 1957, some twenty sites from Arrow Rock, Missouri, to the Santa Fe plaza were eventually accorded registry status and provided with bronze plaques. Moreover three forts that had once played a key role in the trail saga were brought under the management of the National Park Service and made accessible to visitors. Fort Larned and

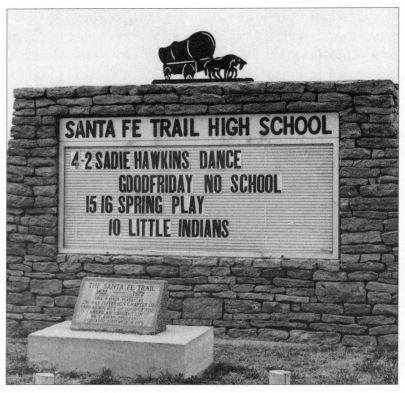

A high school now sits in the ruts of the trail near 110 Mile Crossing, just east of Scranton, Kansas. (author's photo)

Bent's Fort were restored as much as possible to their original appearance, while the ruins of Fort Union were stabilized to protect them from further deterioration.

The states made a contribution by protecting several significant sites, but especially by installing their own interpretive markers at many places that had heretofore been ne-

This marker in the Oklahoma Panhandle, west of Boise City, rests beside fine ruts of the historic trail. (author's photo)

glected. Even individual property owners got into the act. An increasing number in the last twenty years have marked trail sites on their land with homemade signs and have extended a welcome to responsible trail buffs wishing to visit. Farmer Paul Bentrup of Deerfield, Kansas, donated 10 acres of trail ruts adjacent to highway U.S. 50 to the local Kearny County Historical Society for preservation. And Alta Page gave another 110 acres containing the site of Boggsville to the Pioneer Historical Society of Bent County, Colorado. That gift includes a stage station and the house of Tom Boggs, an associate of the Bents and Kit Carson.

Still there continue to be as many setbacks as there are successes. Virtually all the buildings around Independence Square dating from trail days were razed under the misguided urban renewal program of two decades ago. There was even talk of removing the courthouse itself. Though the handsome edifice postdates the trail, it contains some of the structural elements of the 1840s courthouse. The landmark was spared only because of the timely intervention of former President Harry Truman.

In 1980 mountain man Uncle Dick Wootton's two-story adobe house at the top of Raton Pass was demolished by its owner. Four years later the back wall of the Pigeon's Ranch Stage Station, 15 miles east of Santa Fe, collapsed, threatening to bring down the entire building. However, emergency repairs saved the station. A huge block of land condemned in southeastern Colorado for the expansion of Fort Carson included ruins of several splendid stage stations. Not only are the sites now closed to the public, some of the stations have been damaged as a result of tank maneuvers. And in late 1986 fine trail ruts on the eastern outskirts of Santa Fe were swallowed up by bulldozers clearing the land for a new subdivision.

Nevertheless on balance the future of the trail looks brighter than it did even just a few years ago. The beautiful

SANTA FE TRAIL

THIS HIGHWAY FOLLOWS THE OLD SANTA FE TRAIL
USED EXTENSIVELY FROM 1822 BY EARLY PIONEERS
WHO OPENED THE WAY FROM MISSOURI TO SANTA FE.
GEN. S.W. KEARNY'S ARMY OF THE WEST USED THIS
ROUTE TO CONQUER THE SOUTHWEST IN 1846.
NEARBY ARE VISIBLE THE RUTS CUT BY THE HEAVY
OX DRAWN WAGON TRAINS.   COLO. DEPT. OF HIGHWAYS

Santa Fe Trail ruts behind this sign on the plains of Colorado point southwest toward Raton Pass and New Mexico. (author's photo)

Santa Fe Trail Center in Larned, completed in 1974, main-
tains an active program of publicizing and interpreting the
trail. In September of 1986, a trail symposium at Trinidad,
Colorado, resulted in the founding of the Santa Fe Trail
Council (shortly renamed the Santa Fe Trail Association),

Distinctive New Mexico highway marker, on the trail south of Raton Pass. (author's collection)

which proposed to pick up and carry the baton dropped by the original association in the early 1960s. President Ronald Reagan signed a bill in May 1987, designating the Santa Fe Trail a National Historic Trail. And some significant land acquisitions have been made or are proposed by the federal government. As a result of these developments and others, public awareness of the trail is steadily increasing.

Pioneer David Kellogg, traveler to Santa Fe in 1858, camped in eastern Kansas and wrote in his diary: "The glittering stars make night seem enchantment and this, enchanted land."[9] With some consistency chroniclers like Kellogg spoke of the trail in terms of its magical qualities and enchantment. Marian Russell in her recollections referred to its will-o'-the-wisp character as it wound across a strange and wonderous country. And, when her writings appeared in book form, the title taken was *Land of Enchantment*.

After the trail closed in 1880, much of its magic, of course, disappeared. The crawling lines of white-topped wagons and shouting teamsters were gone. The buffalo had been hunted to near extinction, and practically so the antelope. The Indians who had lent both danger and color to a crossing of the prairies were disarmed and confined to distant reservations. Farmers on the eastern wing of the trail were plowing up the still fresh wagon tracks, while cowboys on the western end herded cattle over the campsites where caravans once formed their night circle. Nevertheless in spite of all that was lost and gone with the dry prairie winds, some of the original spell-binding charm of the Santa Fe Trail endured and continues to endure in the Computer Age.

Perhaps that explains a recent resurgence of interest in the history of the trail as well as why lately the number of people who set out to retrace the route grows each year. Most go in comfort by automobile. But some, like participants in the Bicentennial Wagon Train, travel by Conestoga, while

Wagons in Santa Fe plaza, 1867. (Museum of New Mexico, negative no. 144637)

others make the journey on horseback, foot, or even bicycle. From their testimony, we can gather that the enchanted land David Kellogg described and the alluring and wonderous country seen by Marian Russell still exist—out there on the long, long road that reaches from the Missouri River across the miles to an ancient plaza at Santa Fe.

NOTES

1. Mrs. Hal Russell, ed., *Land of Enchantment: Memoirs of Marian Russell along the Santa Fe Trail* (Albuquerque: University of New Mexico Press, 1981), 71.

2. Quoted in W. Somerset Maugham, *Ten Novels and Their Authors* (London: Heinemann Ltd., 1954), 180.

3. *Weekly New Mexican* [Santa Fe], February 14, 1880.

4. *Kansas City Star,* September 1, 1911.

5. J. M. Lowe, *The National Old Trails Road* (Kansas City: privately printed, 1925), 259.

6. Mrs. T. A. Cordry, *The Story of the Marking of the Santa Fe Trail* (Topeka: Crane & Co., 1915), 15.

7. Lalla Maloy Brigham, *The Story of Council Grove on the Santa Fe Trail* (Council Grove: privately printed, 1921), 6.

8. Fern Ioula Bauer, *The Historic Treasure Chest of the Madonna of the Trail Monuments* (Springfield, OH: McEnaney Printing, 1984), 19.

9. David Kellogg, "Across the Plains in 1858," *The Trail* 5 (December 1912): 2.

PART TWO

NEW WORDS
ABOUT AN OLD TRAIL

4

WHITHER BECKNELL?

The following item on William Becknell and his inaugural trip to New Mexico was first published in 1971 to commemorate the 150th anniversary of that event. It presented a new interpretation of Becknell's original design, by showing that his intention from the beginning was to trade with the New Mexicans rather than the Comanches. This revisionist viewpoint has since been accepted by several leading historians.

During the first two decades of the nineteenth century, the province of New Mexico dozed in a remote corner of Spain's colonial empire, shut off from contact with the bumptious Americans to the east by 800 miles of plain and prairie and by royal laws that rigidly forbade commercial contact with foreigners. Young Lieutenant Zebulon Pike, arrested when he strayed into Spanish territory in 1807, prepared a report on his return home that not only won him wide acclaim but awakened interest among American frontiersmen in trade possibilities with New Mexico. But the hostile attitude of the Spanish government discouraged the organization of any formal venture, at least until 1812. At that time revolutionaries in Mexico were engaged in a struggle for independence, and in anticipation of their success, a trading expedition of twelve Americans led by Robert McKnight headed for Santa Fe. Upon their arrival they learned the insurgent forces had been crushed and, since Spain was still firmly in control, they were hustled off to a Chihuahua prison. The rude treatment accorded McKnight's party served as a warning to outsiders, and over the next several years few attempts were made to pierce the Spanish barrier.

On June 25, 1821, Captain William Becknell, a noted Indian fighter and veteran of the War of 1812, placed an advertisement in the *Missouri Intelligencer* seeking the enlistment of seventy men willing to join and invest in an expedition whose purpose was to trade for horses and mules and trap fur-bearing animals "of every description." The destination of the party was left vague, Becknell saying only that he planned to travel westward. By August 4 only five men had applied, but these met, formed a company, and elected Becknell captain of the expedition. They departed from Arrow Rock, Missouri, the following September 1.

Josiah Gregg in his highly regarded *Commerce of the Prairies,* a book written only a few years after the event, declares that the little band started with the original purpose of trading with the Comanches, but having fallen in accidentally with a troop of New Mexicans and learning that Mexico had achieved independence, was easily prevailed upon to con-

Artist Frederick Remington's conception of the first pack train over the Santa Fe Trail. (after Inman)

tinue on to Santa Fe. Accepting this statement at face value, historians invariably have described the Becknell expedition as wandering casually over the plains until a chance meeting with soldiers from Santa Fe revealed that trade restrictions had been removed and Americans were now welcome. Actually there is no truth in any of this, for an assessment of available evidence clearly shows that Captain Becknell intended from the very first to visit the New Mexican settlements.

By the Plan of Iguala, proclaimed on February 24, 1821, Mexico asserted her independence from Spain, although the issue was not fully decided until the following September, when revolutionary forces occupied Mexico City. Thus between February 24 and the following June 25, when Becknell published his advertisement, more than sufficient time had elapsed for news to reach Missouri of the state of Mexican affairs. The strength of the insurgent movement was obviously much greater than it had been nine years before, when Robert McKnight and his companions had made their miscalculation and landed in prison. Another fact might also have encouraged Missourians contemplating a new journey to Santa Fe, and that was the reputation for fairness of Don Facundo Melgares, governor of New Mexico since 1819. Melgares, described by Pike as a man with "a high sense of honor," was known to be friendly toward Americans, and in the crunch the governor's attitude was apt to be more important than restrictive laws. In sum it is apparent that Becknell, while acknowledging the risks, had reason to believe that a bold ride to Santa Fe might succeed in opening a profitable trade. That he failed to state his destination is simply evidence of caution. Had he published his intentions, the word might easily have been picked up by Spanish diplomatic officers in this country and relayed to Mexico.

The journal of Becknell's expedition to New Mexico (printed in the *Missouri Historical Review,* 1910) is brief, unvarnished, and spare in specific details. During the first days traversing the high prairies west of Missouri, the narrative dwells on the sickness and discouragement among the company owing to incessant rain. Beyond the Osage River buffalo were sighted, and one animal was killed to replenish the food supply. Following the Arkansas "meandering very slowly in consequence of the still continued ill health of some of the party," Becknell led his men into southeastern Colorado, thence over Raton Pass, which "presented difficulties almost insurmountable, as we were laboriously engaged nearly two days in rolling away large rocks, before we attempted to get our horses up, and even then one fell and was bruised to death."

Once beyond the pass, the expedition traveled across an open plain to the Canadian River and continued on in a southwesterly direction toward the mountains. The men were now approaching the perimeter of New Mexican settlement, and the journal says, "the prospect of a near termination of our journey excites hope and redoubled exertion, although our horses are so reduced that we only travel from eight to fifteen miles per day." This could scarcely be the statement of a man who was searching for the Comanches, nor does the tone of the account to this point suggest aimless wandering over the plains. From the beginning Becknell clearly had a goal in mind—he was leading his crew in a direct course toward the southwest, and he made no mention in his journal of seeking out Indians to trade. Somewhere east of present Las Vegas, New Mexico, he states "we struck a trail, and found several other indications which induced us to believe the inhabitants had here herded their cattle and sheep." By this time the party was well within the limits of the province and obviously aware of the fact.

Shortly afterward, "on Tuesday morning the 13th [of November], we had the satisfaction of meeting with a party of Spanish troops. Although the difference of our language would not admit of conversation, yet the circumstances attending their reception of us, fully convinced us of their hospitable disposition and friendly feelings." This encounter was accidental enough, but certainly no surprise to Becknell. Nor was there any dramatic announcement that Mexico had won independence and Americans were now welcome. The language barrier precluded any such imparting of news. The expedition had banked on the cordiality of the New Mexicans, and since the amiable attitude of the soldiers was clear enough, the original design to proceed to Santa Fe could now be carried through. Thus there was no invitation on the part of the troops, no sudden alteration in Becknell's plans representing a switch from Indian trading to Mexican trading.

Accompanied by the Spaniards, the Missourians reached the village of San Miguel on the Pecos River the following day, where Becknell found a Frenchman whom he hired as an interpreter. Two days later the party arrived in Santa Fe and "were received with apparent pleasure and joy." Captain Becknell was extended an invitation to visit Governor Melgares whom, he says, "I found to be well-informed and gentlemanly in manner, his demeanor courteous and friendly." Furthermore the governor expressed a desire that Americans keep up contact with his province and "that if any wished to emigrate, it would give him pleasure to afford them every facility."

Plainly, Becknell's gamble had paid off. The small stock of trade goods was disposed of at an enormous profit, and the captain began planning ahead for another and more substantial venture. At least one member of the company chose to remain in New Mexico, but on December 13 Becknell with four companions started home. Evidently anticipating that

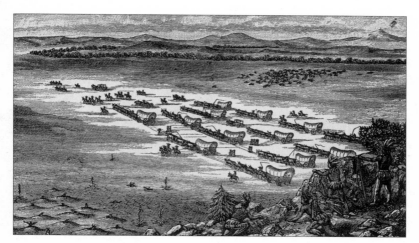

What Beckley set in motion; a caravan of the 1830s. (after Gregg)

his next trip to Santa Fe would be tried with wagons rather than pack mules, he sought out a trail that avoided treacherous Raton Pass, so that his return probably paralleled fairly closely the route that would become the Cimarron Cutoff of the Santa Fe Trail.

Two other parties of Americans reached New Mexico late in 1821 or early the next year. One included Thomas James, who wrote a fanciful account of his experiences in *Three Years among the Indians and Mexicans,* while the other, the Glenn-Fowler company, was composed of mountain men and trappers. But the route pioneered by William Becknell, both on his outgoing and return journeys, was the one destined to become the main trail westward from Missouri. Thus this man well deserves the title bestowed upon him by historian Hiram M. Chittenden, that of "Father of the Santa Fe Trail."

In 1822 Becknell took three wagons to Santa Fe, proving the feasibility of wheeled travel. The success of his enterprize opened the floodgate to imitators, so that by 1824 American merchants realized $190,000 in gross receipts for the year. The budding and first bloom of the Santa Fe trade unfolded during the quarter century New Mexico formed a part of the Mexican Republic. With acquisition of the province by the United States in 1846, traffic, both military and commercial, increased, but some of the old magic disappeared, since Santa Fe was no longer a foreign capital. Mail and stagecoach service was inaugurated and the volume of freight business expanded prodigiously, as contractors hurried to supply the government and private companies with goods.

By the late 1860s, rails were pointing toward the Rio Grande, but it was not until 1878 that the Santa Fe Railroad surmounted Raton Pass. Two years later when tracks reached Lamy, station for the New Mexican capital, a local newspaper reported in bold type: "The Old Santa Fe Trail Passes into Oblivion." The adventure begun by William Becknell six decades before had come to an end.

NOTE

When Captain William Becknell reached Santa Fe in November 1821, Governor Facundo Melgares made it clear the old trade restrictions imposed by Spain had been removed by the newly independent Mexican government. Did the governor receive some special directive on this matter from his superiors, allowing him to open New Mexico's doors to American merchants? A search of the Mexican Archives of New Mexico in Santa Fe has turned up no such document. Discovered, however, were two printed circulars issued from Mexico City about mid-1821 to all provincial officers. The title of the first reads: "General Interim Tariff and Instruction for the Maritime Customs Houses in the Free Commerce of the Mexican Empire." Although not applying to New Mexico, since the province had no seaport, the reference to free commerce is significant. The second document, "Manifesto of the Provisional Governing Junta, 1821," contains a specific clause on the subject of trade, which in itself would have been sufficient to permit Governor Melgares to welcome William Becknell and other Americans. The clause declares:

The measures which the Junta has proposed in order to guarantee and extend our independence are, in addition to rallying the people, the alliance, association, and commerce with other nations. . . . With respect to foreign nations, we shall maintain harmony with all, commercial relations, and whatever else may be appropriate.

5

THE SANTA FE TRAIL AS
HIGH ADVENTURE

WALTER PRESCOTT WEBB, upon assuming the office of president of the American Historical Association in 1958, delivered an acceptance address entitled, "History as High Adventure." In his remarks he spoke of historical explorers who personally experience adventures in the great wilderness of the past. That exploration, he said, "is as exciting as any known to argonauts or *conquistadores.*"[1]

While Webb was speaking of history in general, I think he would have acknowledged, had the question been put to him, that historical periods and subjects vary enormously in their potential for adventure. The Civil War, for instance, raises enthusiasm in legions of scholars and writers, amateurs and well as professionals. The Era of Reconstruction, however, inspires no such outpouring of zeal.

One chapter of American history that has long offered a productive arena for those dedicated to adventuring in the past is the story of the frontier. The Indian, the mountain man, the cowboy, the pioneer mother, the cavalryman, and the desert prospector represent some of the most popular images deriving from that phase of our national history. They have been depicted in literature, song, and film, but unfortunately not always with strict fidelity to historical truth.

Here I wish to draw upon Webb and recast the title of his acceptance address to provide a heading for my own remarks. In taking the subject, "The Santa Fe Trail as High Adventure," my intention is to use it as a vehicle in attempting to explain why so many people today seem fascinated by the trail and also to show how trail study can be an exciting and valuable experience. In a larger sense, I will be giving an example of the utility and worth of history.

To begin it might be well to ask: what did the idea of adventure mean to original travelers on the Santa Fe Trail? And to what degree was adventure a motive in luring them to undertake the perilous and difficult journey overland to New Mexico?

The question of motive is perhaps easiest to answer. It is well documented that the men who entered the Santa Fe trade did so in a quest for profit. William Becknell, who inaugurated the commerce between Missouri and New Mexico in 1821, was deeply in debt, and his bold first ride across poorly known plains and mountains had about it the air of a desperate gamble.[2] When it paid off, with the quick sale of his mule loads of merchandise to the Mexican citizens of Santa Fe, others were inspired to follow both his trail and his example. The first wave of would-be merchants was made up of small farmers, poor tradesmen, and even border vagabonds who, as Becknell had done, were able to borrow a couple of hundred dollars to get them into the overland trade.

Later, of course, as the value of commerce with Santa Fe ballooned, well-capitalized individuals and firms took command of the trade with Mexico and squeezed out many of the small marginal merchants who had helped launch the far-flung business. This occurred in the headlong pursuit of greater profits.

While the profit motive has long been recognized as the spark that ignited the "commerce of the prairies," it must be acknowledged that something else—the lure of high adventure—fueled the desire of many to remain year after year in the overland trade in spite of monumental hazards and the inevitable loss of some cargos. The Santa Fe merchants were risk takers, and the facing of great odds on the trail for them held considerable appeal.

That the merchants were responding as much to adventure's call as they were to the opportunity to reap financial rewards is a circumstance not immediately apparent. That is because the motive of adventure must be inferred through a careful reading between the lines in the original chronicles and diaries of the trade's participants. Josiah Gregg, who launched his own commercial career in the early 1830s, informs us by way of example that in roving over this picturesque caravan trail he developed "a passion for Prairie travel" and for "the wild, unsettled and independent life of the Prairie trader . . ."[3]

In essence what Gregg is saying is that he had become enamored of the high adventure that was part of every wagon

Josiah Gregg, chief chronicler of the trail. (Museum of New Mexico, no. 9896)

trip to New Mexico. In the eight crossings he is known to have made over the southern prairies, there is no evidence that he became rich through merchandising. In his case at least, it was not the promise of profits that drew him on, but the prospect of adventure.

Among the majority of merchants, however, there probably existed a mixture of motives, so it is proper to declare that the hunger for profit and the thirst for adventure were the twin pillars upon which the Santa Fe trade was founded and upon which it flourished for six decades.

The same could also be said for other categories of travelers who appeared on the trail in the latter stages of its history. Some of the forty-niners, for instance, chose to follow the southern route, beginning with the Santa Fe Trail, rather than the northern route that used a portion of the Oregon Trail, on their way to the California goldfields. Clearly these were men wedded to the hope of getting rich quick, but they must also have been endowed with a taste for adventuring. Otherwise they would have tried their hands at tamer pursuits nearer home.

Charles Pancoast was one of these fortune hunters, and he joined a company that took the Santa Fe Trail because it was said that grass for livestock was more abundant on that route. In the book containing his recollections, *A Quaker Forty-Niner,* he vividly described the make up of his caravan, indicating that it contained a cross section of American society as it existed in the mid-nineteenth century.

Our Train was composed of forty-four Teams, . . . There were in all two hundred men, natives of different States and Countries. The Characters and Dispositions of the men varied much. There were ignorant and learned; generous and selfish; indolent and industrious; wild and erratic, and staid sober Souls; jubilant good Fellows, and crooked ill-natured Curmudgeons. There were Preachers, Doctors,

*Lawyers, Druggists, Pilots, Mechanics, Farmers, Laborers, Sailors,
and representatives of many occupations. Among them was a three
hundred-pound Pilot. Some of the men were as old as sixty-five years;
others were invalid when they started.4*

From what the historical record reveals about the gold-
rush mentality, it is a safe assumption that all of these individuals of diverse background were united in a common desire to reach the diggings and find a fortune. But secondarily
they were drawn westward over dangerous trails by the
prospect of high adventure.

In the spring of 1858 Julia Archibald Holmes and her husband joined the first Kansas party of Pike's Peakers traveling
the Santa Fe Trail to the new gold strikes in Colorado. From
her writings it is evident that Julia was more interested in
new experiences and excitement associated with the journey
than she was in any will-o'-the-wisp gold mines that might
wait at the end of the trail. At Cottonwood Creek in eastern Kansas, she described "the grandeur of the scene" as she
beheld "the great, silent, uninhabited plains."

*With the blue sky overhead, the endless variety of flowers under foot, it
seemed that the ocean's solitude had united with all the landscape
beauties. In such a scene there is a peculiar charm for some minds, which
it is impossible for me to describe; but it made my heart leap for joy.5*

In Julia Holmes's case, the adventurous aspects of trail life
unquestionably took precedence over the quest for wealth.

Another excellent illustration of the way high adventure

Marian Sloan Russell, at age 46. (author's collection)

influenced impressionable trail travelers can be found in the experiences of Marian Sloan Russell and her mother Eliza Sloan. They made a series of plains crossings in the 1850s and 1860s, and late in life Marian recorded the details in her dictated memoirs. As motive for their wanderings, she says only that her mother had become a nomad, "who gaily betook herself back and forth over the trail on first one pretext and then another."[6] Of her travels on the Santa Fe Trail, Mrs. Sloan once told Kit Carson, "It is rough I know, and maybe dangerous, . . . but I love it."[7]

In this case the desire for profit played no part at all in launching the two women on their many trips over the trail. For them the adventure was everything. It was even sufficient to override all the discomforts, hardships, and perils that beset every caravan bound for Santa Fe. "The old, old trail," Marian proclaimed, "like a rainbow, led us westward."[8] And in reflecting upon those early days, she recalled a childhood vow: "When I grew up, I said to myself, I would travel endlessly back and forth over the Santa Fe Trail. I loved the trail and would live always on it."[9]

From even this sketchy evidence, it should be clear that high adventure was part and parcel of life with the Santa Fe caravans. Indeed some of that spirit of adventure can still be found on the trail today, although its character and tone are of a different order. Most of what happened in the way of wagon journeys, Indian attacks, buffalo stampedes, and prairie fires are things that belonged to another era and cannot come again. But adventure exists in many forms, so that for those who are imaginative and persistent, the Santa Fe Trail yet offers the excitement of challenge and discovery.

As a preliminary step to modern-day adventuring, however, some effort must be exerted to master the trail's story, by way of background. That is best done through reading—by studying and assimilating a portion of the mountain of trail literature. General histories are useful for the beginner, such as those by Duffus, Vestal, and Connor and Skaggs.[10] But the real essence and flavor of the trail lie in the firsthand diaries, journals, and reports of people, famous and obscure, who made the trek by ox train to the far Southwest and therein recorded their experiences. By means of their individual histories, we come to know them as actual persons and to see the trail adventure in all its dimensions. The published accounts of people like Josiah Gregg, Matt Field, Susan Magoffin, and Lewis H. Garrard, to name a few, contain that inner glow that stimulates the imagination and allow one to recreate in the mind's eye a picture of those far-off days when covered freight wagons rolled by the hundreds across the southern plains to New Mexico and beyond.[11]

What occurs here, as in the study of all history, is well summed up in a quote from Winston Churchill. While he knew nothing of the Santa Fe Trail, his words, nevertheless, are particularly applicable, the more so perhaps because he uses the felicitous phrase, "the trail of the past." Here is his statement, which possesses the quality of epigram: "History with its flickering lamp stumbles along the trail of the past, trying to reconstruct its scenes, to revive its echoes, and kindle with pale gleams the passion of former days."[12] In their own search for high adventure, present-day trail travelers, armed with the knowledge gained from the printed page, become engaged in reconstructing scenes that focus on white-topped prairie schooners and in reviving the echoes of rumbling wagon wheels in a process of re-creation on the road to Santa Fe.

Once the outline of the trail's compelling story has been grasped—when we know how the trail was opened and under what circumstances, and the way the Santa Fe trade evolved and flourished, and how it eventually ended with the advance of the railroad—then we are ready for our next step along the highway to adventure. And that step involves seeing the country firsthand, meeting the trail, or what's left of it, face to face.

Armed with historical knowledge, today's travelers can set forth with full confidence that their explorations will yield abundant opportunities for adventure. Most people will go by automobile, but a few, hoping to recapture something more of the pioneer spirit, elect to journey by foot, horseback, or wagon. Whatever the means of locomotion, serious explorers will easily find the major landmarks, stopping places, and battle sites where the wagons formed a circle and fought off Indians. With the facts of history as part of our mental baggage, we are able to conjure up a picture of past events at each location and in so doing resurrect them from their burial in books and give them new life. In combining historical knowledge with personal experience, we have created a formula for high adventure.

At a place such as Pawnee Rock, the best known landmark in central Kansas, the informed visitor has access to a flood of material for picture forming. Virtually every wagon train and stagecoach bound for New Mexico passed under the shadow of the rock. The level plain below the south face was a favorite camping site, acreage that is now sown in wheat. Innumerable ambushes were carried out here by hos-

Pawnee Rock, Kansas. A wheat field now covers the wagon campground at its base. (Courtesy of Allan Maybee)

tile Indians, and the prairie sod conceals the unmarked graves of those who fell victim to arrows or bullets.

From the summit early traders had a peerless view of the teeming herds of buffalo and antelope that stretched eastward to the Great Bend of the Arkansas and westward toward Ash Creek and Pawnee Fork. And something more. Of Pawnee Rock, Josiah Gregg observed that "upon its surface are furrowed, in uncouth but legible characters, numerous dates, and the names of various travelers who have chanced to pass that way."[13] Kit Carson, Susan Magoffin, and perhaps Gregg himself left their inscriptions in the company of hundreds of others. But nearly all have disappeared with the ravages of time.

Along the thousand-mile length of the trail from Franklin, Missouri, to Santa Fe remain scores of other landmarks and sites scarcely less storied than Pawnee Rock: among them Fort Osage, Independence Square, Council Grove, Diamond Spring, Plum Buttes, Cimarron Crossing, Point of Rocks, the Rabbit Ears, Raton Pass, Wagon Mound, San Miguel del Vado, and the Santa Fe plaza. Those with an eye for adventure can find in such places the echoes of human drama unparalleled in the history of the American West.

In exploring the trail and reaching backward to span the years, we gain a larger sense of community, as the lives of pioneer travelers help clarify our nation's identity and roots. The parameters of adventure on the Santa Fe Trail are surely broader than I have sketched here, but perhaps enough has been said to suggest that by following that unwinding road leading south by southwest, unexpected discoveries and high excitement await those yet responsive to the lure of history.

1. Walter Prescott Webb, *History as High Adventure* (Austin: Pemberton Press, 1969), 4.

2. Larry M. Beachum, *William Becknell, Father of the Santa Fe Trade* (El Paso: Texas Western Press, 1982), 16–18.

3. Paul Horgan, *Josiah Gregg and His Vision of the Early West* (New York: Farrar Straus Giroux, 1979), 31–32.

4. Anna Paschall Hannum, ed., *A Quaker Forty-Niner: The Adventures of Charles Edward Pancoast* (Philadelphia: University of Pennsylvania Press, 1930), 184–85.

5. Julia Archibald Holmes, *A Bloomer Girl on Pike's Peak,* ed. by Agnes Wright Spring (Denver: Denver Public Library, 1949), 15.

6. Mrs. Hal Russell, *Land of Enchantment: Memoirs of Marian Russell along the Santa Fe Trail* (Albuquerque: University of New Mexico Press, 1981), 87.

7. Russell, *Land of Enchantment,* 86.

8. Russell, *Land of Enchantment,* 15.

9. Russell, *Land of Enchantment,* 70.

10. Robert L. Duffus, *The Santa Fe Trail* (Albuquerque: University of New Mexico Press, 1979); Stanley Vestal, *The Old Santa Fe Trail* (Boston: Houghton Mifflin, 1939); Seymour V. Connor and Jimmy M. Skaggs, *Broadcloth and Britches: The Santa Fe Trade* (College Station, TX: A & M University Press, 1977).

11. Josiah Gregg, *Commerce of the Prairies,* ed. by Max L. Moorhead (Norman: University of Oklahoma Press, 1954); John E. Sunder, ed., *Matt Field on the Santa Fe Trail* (Norman: University of Oklahoma Press, 1960); Stella M. Drumm, ed., *Down the Santa Fe Trail and into Mexico: The Diary of Susan Shelby Magoffin* (Lincoln: University of Nebraska Press, 1966); Lewis H. Garrard, *Wah-to-*

yah and the Taos Trail (Norman: University of Oklahoma Press, 1974).

12. Quoted in Samuel Eliot Morison, *Vistas of History* (New York: Alfred A. Knopf, 1964), 21.

13. Gregg, *Commerce of the Prairies,* 42.

6

PECOS PUEBLO ON THE
SANTA FE TRAIL

THERE IS ONE historic place in New Mexico that I keep returning to again and again. It is the ruined pueblo and Spanish mission of Pecos in the foothills of the Sangre de Cristos, twenty-five miles east of Santa Fe.

I have been there at all seasons of the year and in every kind of weather. No visit is ever quite the same.

Once on Christmas Eve, many years ago, I attended a wedding in the old roofless church. Friends from Santa Fe brought a justice of the peace and had him perform the ceremony from the adobe platform that had once held a stone altar.

Afterward the wedding party, with the JP in tow, piled into cars and returned to Santa Fe, where a local bar had been reserved for the reception. In the course of the evening, the bartender happened to hear that the nuptials had been celebrated at Pecos ruins.

"Oh, that's not possible," he exclaimed. "The old pueblo is just across the line in San Miguel County and your JP has no jurisdiction there." To make things legal, the Justice obligingly went through the ceremony again, there in the bar.

All of this I learned later, since I had stayed behind at Pecos to wander alone through the acres of fallen stone houses. As the evening darkened, flakes of snow began to tumble quietly into the ancient plaza. It was a good time to feel the presence of all the ghosts of Indians and Spaniards who had lived there in centuries past.

When Coronado stopped at Pecos in the spring of 1541, the pueblo was one of the largest and most imposing Indian villages in New Mexico. Castaño de Sosa and his expedition, passing by in late 1590, found the people hostile and took the place by storm after a furious battle.

With the permanent colonization of New Mexico in 1598, friars began conversion of the Pecos people. The huge and splendid mission church, which took a number of years to build, was destroyed in the great Pueblo Revolt of 1680. And when the Spaniards took up work at Pecos again, they built an entirely new church on the ruins of the old.

New Mexico's Governor Juan Bautista de Anza met the Comanches at Pecos in 1786. In a showy ceremony, he concluded a treaty of peace with the tribe that lasted far into the next century.

As Americans began moving west over the Santa Fe Trail after 1821, they found Pecos in a mournful condition. Years of warfare with hostile Plains tribes and a series of epidemics

Ruins of Pecos Pueblo (left) and mission (right), soon after abandonment. Caravans camped on flats at center. (Museum of New Mexico, engraving no. 6504)

had reduced the population to a mere handful. The old mission and many house blocks, after ages of neglect, were beginning to fall apart. By 1838 the few survivors abandoned their decaying village and moved west to Jemez Pueblo, where they were made welcome.

By the time archeologists began serious work at Pecos in 1915, the remains of the pueblo were hidden under mounds of earth, and the church walls were more than half gone. In 1966 the National Park Service took over the site and it became Pecos National Monument.

Much has been written about the pueblo by those who have dug in the ruins and those who have searched the archives for documents telling of the Spanish activity there. However, one phase of Pecos history has not received much attention: its role as a major campsite and attraction on the Santa Fe Trail.

From the opening of the trail in 1821 down to its close in 1880, Pecos had a steady stream of visitors—merchants from Missouri at first, then later soldiers, California emigrants, and stagecoach passengers.

On the flats surrounding the pueblo could be found an abundance of wood, water, and grass, the essentials for a comfortable camp. If a caravan got a good rest at Pecos, it could usually make Santa Fe with another hard day's push.

Following the evening meal, travelers wandered through the ruins seeing the sights. The deserted rooms and church and the eerie silence made a lasting impression on many of them, and they often recorded their observations in trail journals or in letters home.

Because next to nothing was then known about the history of Pecos, people engaged in wild speculation. At a very early date, a story was started that the Aztec emperor Montezuma had resided there. Departing for the south one day, he instructed the inhabitants to keep a sacred fire burning until he should return. The trust had been kept and the fire fed, generation after generation, until desertion of the village in 1838.

When Matthew Field passed by in 1839, an old sheepherder told him the story. He gave the man a "few bits of silver" and in return was given a "genuine" cinder from the

One of the last of the Pecos Indians. (after Twitchell)

sacred fire, extinguished only the year before. It was probably the first curio purchased by a tourist at Pecos.

The Montezuma legend, in numerous versions, was
recorded again and again by travelers. Josiah Gregg had
much to say about the tale, and Pecos itself, in his classic

account of the trail, *Commerce of the Prairies,* first published in 1844.

He also recorded another popular story associated with the ruins, that of a giant snake god. The Indians were supposed to have kept it in a cave back of the pueblo and fed their own infants to it. Gregg noted that some superstitious souls credited the decline of the village to the huge appetite of the snake. "The story of this wonderful serpent was firmly believed in by many ignorant people," he said.

In 1843, the year before Gregg's book appeared, famed historian William H. Prescott had published his monumental *The Conquest of Mexico.* Widely read in the United States, it first brought the attention of the reading public to the stirring events surrounding Montezuma's encounter with Cortez and the overthrow of the Aztec empire.

Montezuma, thus, may have been fresh in the minds of the American soldiers who stopped at Pecos in mid-August 1846, on their way to the conquest of Santa Fe. Some among them were excited to hear that the old Aztec had once inhabited this forsaken ruin, and they recorded the "fact" in their diaries.

Eighteen-year-old Susan Magoffin spoke of it too, but with a measure of scepticism. She was traveling in a trade caravan directly behind the conquering army.

"The ancient pueblo is now desolate and a home for the wild beasts," wrote Susan. "Here tis said the great Montezuma once lived, though tis probably a false tradition, as the most learned American historians report that the great monarch resided much farther south than any portion of New Mexico."

Not long after the United States acquired the Southwest, regular stagecoach service was inaugurated over the Santa Fe Trail. The coaches did not stop overnight at Pecos, but sometimes they would pause long enough for passengers to explore the ruins.

When his stage did just that, in the summer of 1853, young William W. H. Davis got out for a look around. He was the newly appointed territorial attorney on his way from Missouri to his new duties in Santa Fe.

Becoming engrossed in a tour of the old pueblo, Davis forgot the time. When he looked around, the stage had gone, and he had a hard run of over half a mile before he caught up with it.

In the latter 1850s, a Pole named Martin Kozlowski, who had earlier come to New Mexico with the army, settled on the Pecos River about a mile southeast of the ruins. Kozlowski's Ranch became a favorite lunch stop for the stagecoaches. Indeed some claimed that the best meal between Independence and Santa Fe was to be had there. Mrs. Kozlowski served up enormous piles of food, including fried trout snatched fresh from the river at the ranch's back door.

Kozlowski's, much remodeled and later expanded, became the headquarters for the Forked Lightning Ranch, owned by Colonel E. E. Fogelson and his wife, actress Greer Garson.

Today deep trail ruts, filled with weeds and sunflowers,

can be seen just south of the ruins. These wheel traces are some of the most interesting features to be found at Pecos, now classified as a National Historical Park. They represent physical artifacts left from the days when the great freight wagons and stagecoaches rolled by.

7

BERNARD SELIGMAN:
JEWISH MERCHANT ON THE TRAIL

In THE PERIOD after 1850, a number of Jewish immigrants from Germany entered the Santa Fe trade, freighting over the trail from Missouri and becoming prominent in the economic and political life of New Mexico. A leading example of such men was Bernard Seligman.

Born near the Rhine River on November 23, 1837, Bernard Seligman received a good education and learned to speak six languages fluently. Before leaving Germany, he was associated with the great banking house of the Rothschilds at Frankfort-on-the-Main. After coming to the United States, he located briefly in the Philadelphia area, where he was involved in the manufacture of cotton goods.[1]

In 1856 Bernard, not yet twenty, went west and traveled the Santa Fe Trail to New Mexico. He was going to join his older brother, Sigmund, who had settled in Santa Fe in 1849 and since that year had been active in merchandising. Sigmund Seligman, then forty-three, had formed a partnership in 1855 with another German Jew, Charles P. Cleaver, from Cologne. Their firm was known as Seligman & Cleaver, which was said to have "engaged extensively in a flourishing trade over the Santa Fe Trail."[2]

Young Bernard went to work for the company and by 1862 was a full partner. By then Cleaver had withdrawn, going on to a career in law and politics, and the firm took the name Seligman Bros. One of their many advertisements in the local *Santa Fe New Mexican,* dated December 5, 1863, conveys an idea of the nature of their business:

Look Here! Look Here!
The place to get good bargains is at Seligman Bros. We are continually receiving by express from New York and other eastern cities and have continually on hand every description of staple and fancy dry goods: Domestics, calicos, cloaks, mantillas, boots, shoes, hats, caps, hardware, groceries, stationery, etc. etc.[3]

It is known that Bernard was in New York in 1866, probably making purchases for the firm and arranging for their shipment to the head of the Santa Fe Trail in Missouri.[4] How many other trips he may have made in these years is unknown. Thus far no diaries or journals of Bernard's trail travels have come to light.

One item of record notes that Seligman Brothers loaded in one day in Kansas City eighty-three wagons with an average of 5,000 pounds each for their store in Santa Fe, which at times carried in stock as much as $200,000 worth of merchandise. A freight bill of $30,000 was paid by the firm to one wagon train carrying $125,000 worth of their goods. This delivery was sold within three weeks upon arrival at the Santa Fe store, and the profit made on that single consignment was $51,000. Total sales of $10 million were reported to have been reached during the life of the company.[5]

From this it would appear that the Seligmans relied primarily upon private contractors to transport their freight to New Mexico. This was clearly the case by the early 1870s, when the Kansas Pacific Railway reached Kit Carson, Colorado, the latest trail head for wagon traffic to Santa Fe. Surviving bills of lading and invoices indicate that Otero, Sellar & Co., commission and forwarding merchants, was receiving consignments of goods destined for Seligman Bros. and freighting them to the New Mexican capital.

Some of the wares carried, as revealed in these documents, were clothing, stationery, carpets, tobacco, cheese, vinegar, mace, pepper, oils, buckets, tubs, washboards, lampwicks, and barrels and half-barrels of whiskey. One shipment also included two ox yokes and wagon covers.[6] In 1872 the Seligmans had a government contract to supply grain to Indian agencies in the Southwest, and the yokes and covers may have been intended for the use of their delivery wagons.[7]

Both Seligman brothers took an active role in the civic life of the Santa Fe community. As early as 1859, Bernard, along with his good friend Zadoc Staab, joined with other municipal leaders to found the Historical Society of New Mexico, the first such organization west of the Mississippi.[8] An accomplished public speaker, Bernard soon gained po-

Bernard Seligman *(left)* and friends Zadoc Staab and Lehman Speigelberg with Kiowa Indians. (Museum of New Mexico, negative no. 7890)

litical influence and served in both houses of the territorial legislature. He was also treasurer of the territory from 1886 to 1891. Sigmund devoted most of his time to the business, although he was appointed a Santa Fe county commissioner in 1876, the year of his death.[9]

Before the first bank was chartered in Santa Fe, in 1870, Seligman Bros., in addition to its mercantile activities, engaged in private banking. That was a valuable service for Santa Fe freighters and others, who were accustomed to carrying thousands of dollars on their persons. The firm also helped finance construction of the Denver and Rio Grande Railroad.[10]

At the end of his life, Bernard Seligman returned to live in Philadelphia, where he died on February 3, 1903. He left a wife and four children. His son Arthur, born at Santa Fe in 1871, had entered the family business as a bookkeeper in his youth and took over its management upon the retirement of his father. He served as mayor of Santa Fe, 1910–12, and two terms as state governor, from 1930 to 1933.[11]

Arthur Seligman had two interesting connections with the Santa Fe Trail. First as mayor of Santa Fe he participated in the dedication ceremonies of the DAR "End of the Trail" marker on the Santa Fe plaza, August 21, 1911, accepting it on behalf of the city.

Second he acquired the last surviving Barlow and Sanderson stagecoach that had traveled the trail in the 1860s and 1870s. It was the one involved in a famous holdup on Raton Pass in 1867 by the Kid Barton gang. The express messenger and two passengers had been killed and $60,000 taken. Lawmen pursued the gang and in a shoot-out a sheriff and two deputies were slain. But Kid Barton was captured and hanged.

Arthur Seligman for many years rode in the coach during Santa Fe parades and pageants. In 1935, two years after his death, it was presented by his widow to the Historical Society of New Mexico. Today it remains on display in the historic Governors Palace on the Santa Fe plaza.[12]

NOTES

1. Biographical sketch of Bernard Seligman in Ralph Emerson Twitchell, *Old Santa Fe* (Danville, Illinois: Interstate Printers, 1925), 477.

2. Quoted in "Obituary of Arthur Seligman," *New Mexico Historical Review* 8 (October 1933): 306. For a sketch of Charles P. Cleaver, see Floyd S. Fierman, *Guts and Ruts: The Jewish Pioneer on the Trail in the American Southwest* (New York: KTAV Publ. House, 1985), 66–85.

3. From a microfilm copy in the New Mexico State Records Center and Archives, Santa Fe (NMSRCA).

4. His presence in New York is mentioned in *Seligman vs Baca,* 1866, District Court, Mora County, Civil Case #37a, in NMSRCS.

5. Figures are from an original advertising circular, undated, issued by Seligman Bros. Co., in possession of the author.

6. Bills of lading, dated August 17 and November 4, 1872, in Seligman Papers, NMSRCA.

7. See for example Receipts for delivery of corn and wheat to Agency at Fort Defiance, Arizona, May 25, 1872, in Seligman papers, NMSRCA.

8. Jacqueline Dorgan Meketa, *Louis Felsenthal* (Albuquerque: University of New Mexico Press, 1982), 20.

9. *Daily New Mexican,* March 14, 1876.

10. "Obituary of Arthur Seligman," 306–7.

11. Twitchell, *Old Santa Fe,* 477–78.

12. The story of the coach is related in Boaz Long, "Stagecoach Traveling," *El Palacio* 60 (December 1953): 403–8.

THE POETRY
OF THE SANTA FE TRAIL

SOMEONE ONCE SAID that there is poetry in the story of old trails—in their history, in the country through which they passed, and in the lives and adventures of people who traveled them. If true that would help explain why so many persons who have come in contact with the historic Santa Fe Trail have chosen to write poems about it. Their ranks include the likes of Sharlot Hall, Arizona's poet laureate; western novelest Eugene Manlove Rhodes; New Mexico's renowned cowboy poet S. Omar Barker; and even the distinguished American writer Vachel Lindsay.

The majority of the verse about the Santa Fe Trail, however, has been turned out by rank amateurs, by individuals who became caught up in the spirit of the trail. In its drama, its color, romance, tragedy, and humor they found a fit subject for creative effort. The quality of the poems ranges from artfully crafted gems to pure doggerel, but all of it can be described as sincere in sentiment. Of the quantity, no one can say with certainty, except that scores of trail poems are known, and many more may exist, as yet undiscovered.

The span of years the Santa Fe Trail was in existence (1821–80) coincided with the "Age of Poetry," a time in the nineteenth century when verse filled the columns of newspapers and magazines and new books of poems were announced almost daily by publishers. Great national events such as the Mexican War and the Civil War, as well as the individual adventure of crossing the western prairies in a covered wagon elicited a great outpouring of popular poetry. All were encouraged to join in its writing, and many accepted the invitation and did.

The earliest poem so far known that deals with the Santa Fe Trail was published in the *Missouri Intelligencer,* November 6, 1829. According to an editorial note, it represented a eulogy to the memory of a young merchant, Samuel Craig Lamme, "who fell lately in an attack made by a party of Indians on his caravan, while on the prairie trace between Missouri and Santa Fe."[1] It seems that Lamme with two companions left the wagon train to scout ahead, soon after crossing the Arkansas River in western Kansas on the Cimarron Cutoff. They were shortly set upon by Kiowas. In fleeing Lamme fell behind, because he was riding a mule, while the others had horses. He was overtaken, killed, and scalped.

The first verse of the poem to this young man reads:

> No sculptured marble marks the grave,
> Where your remains, brave youth, are laid;

Nor drooping willows, pensive weave,
Around the spot, their humble shade.

It is a typical sentimental poem of the day, worth recalling only because it may, indeed, have been the first dealing with the subject of the trail.

In the decade that followed, the 1830s, two young men traveled to Santa Fe, both of whom wrote numbers of poems derived from their experiences. They were Albert Pike and Matt Field. Their poetry and other writings have recently been reprinted, but the poems are only of antiquarian interest, having no value as either literature or history.[2]

Over the years poems of the trail flowed forth in a steady stream. Some of them were about famous places along the route, such as Independence, Council Grove, and Santa Fe. Others were written to commemorate notable incidents. For example an English nobleman, Lord Frederick Haxby, happened to be at Fort Dodge in 1868, when four troopers, who had been carrying the mail to Fort Larned, were brought in wounded. They had been surrounded at Little Coon Creek and for hours had fought off large numbers of attacking Indians.

His Lordship was so impressed by their tale of heroism that in their honor he composed "The Ballad of Little Coon Creek." It was widely printed in newspapers, both in America and Great Britain. In fact the ballad's popularity may have contributed to the four soldiers later being awarded the Congressional Medal of Honor.[3]

Another poem, this one about tragedy rather than heroism, was written to tell of the death of a young nun, Sister Mary Alphonsa Thompson, who perished in a well-known incident of 1867, while crossing the plains to New Mexico in the company of Bishop John B. Lamy. Above the Arkansas Crossing in Kansas, the wagon caravan to which the bishop's party was attached suffered a furious assault by several hundred Comanches.

After the enemy had been repulsed, the bishop wrote in his journal: "The youngest Sister of Loretto [Mary Alphonsa] died, on the 24th of July, from fright, as I considered it, caused by the attack of the savages. She was eighteen years of age, well educated, and a model of virtue." Actually the good sister had been suffering from cholera, but the terror occasioned by the noise of battle may have pushed her over the edge.

Afterward a Catholic poet, Eleanor Donnelly, wrote about the sister's death in a poem that came to be loved by every Lorettine and was familiar to the pupils in their schools, including the one that existed, until recently, in Santa Fe. The opening verse begins:

> They made her a grave where the tall grasses wave,
> 'Neath the blue of the Western sky,
> And they laid her to sleep where the wild waves sweep,
> Through the bending reeds that sigh.
> With a swelling heart they were forced to part
> A link from that sacred chain,
> And though lovely and bright, it was laid at night,
> 'Neath the sods on the Western plain.[4]

Reenactment scene, 1902, of the burial of Sister Mary Alphonsa Thompson, who died on the trail in 1867. (Museum of New Mexico, negative no. 67741)

There exists a curious aftermath to the episode. Somehow word was carried from the plains that the bishop's train had been overcome by the Comanches. Papers in the East and in Europe carried stories proclaiming that the bishop with his priests and nuns had been killed and mutilated. Weeks later, when Lamy and his party arrived at the small settlement of Trinidad, at the foot of Raton Pass, they were astonished to read the lurid tale of their massacre in an old issue of the Denver *Gazette* and to hear that the local priest had sung a requiem mass for their souls.[5]

Preserving the memory of events through verse seems to have been inborn in many pioneer Americans. Take an instance recorded by Senator James R. Doolittle, who headed a commission that traveled the Santa Fe Trail in 1865 to investigate Indian affairs following the Sand Creek Massacre. As the senator's party arrived at the summit of Raton Pass, he wrote: "When at length we reached the line of New Mexico many a shout and cheer went up with an occasional apostrophe—now in prose and now in rhyme—now to the enormous territories we had just traveled through and now to the greater one we were just entering."[6] In other words, as he tells us, someone authored a poem to mark the passage of the company into a new land.

The practice of honoring the Santa Fe Trail through poems continued well into the twentieth century, long after the trail had closed. Numbers of them were published in the Atchison, Topeka and Santa Fe Railroad Company's periodical, the *Santa Fe Trail Magazine*. An example that appeared in a 1913 issue was entitled "The Famous Old Trail," by Iona Cahill. The first verse went:

> From Missouri's turbid stream
> To the old post, Santa Fe,
> In a long unbroken sea,
> Runs a scarred and rutted way,
> Ling'ring 'round which many a tale
> Lives to mark the famous trail.[7]

While there is nothing remarkable in a literary way about this and similar poems, they do represent an interesting expression of nostalgia that many writers have felt toward the old road to Santa Fe.

That nostalgia, together with an air of mystery, emerges in these lines penned by Santa Fe poet Arthur Chapman in the 1920s.

And when the night has drawn its veil
The teams plod, span on span,
And one sees o'er the long dead trail
A ghostly caravan.[8]

One of the best known poems of the trail, composed by James Grafton Rogers, was called simply, "The Santa Fe Trail." Its popularity stems from the fact that it was set to music and has been recorded on several occasions. It opens with the familiar lines:

Say, pard! Have ye sighted a schooner,
A hittin' the Santa Fe Trail?
They made it here Monday or sooner
With a water keg roped on the tail,
With daddy and ma on the mule seat,
And somewhere around on the way,
A tow-headed girl on a pony,
A-jinglin' for old Santa Fe—
A-jinglin' for old Santa Fe.[9]

Here, as in the other examples given, one senses that adventure, excitement, and romance have colored the memory of the trail and cast a mythic glow over its history.

Even the most casual reading into America's past will suggest that moving west or southwest by covered wagon was an experience filled with danger, hardship, and discomfort. Still the evidence found in contemporary diaries and journals and in recollections set down later would indicate that many of the participants remembered their journey to Santa Fe as an exhilarating time in their lives.

Marian Sloan Russell, who first went to New Mexico as a child in the 1850s, wrote when she was in her nineties living in the Stonewall Valley of Colorado, that "My life as I look back seems to have been lived best in those days on the trail." And she added, "There have been many things that I have striven to forget, but not those journeys over the old trail. The lure it held for us! Seems the folks who made those trips in covered wagons never forgot them."[10] While she did not render her feelings in verse, she did speak in poetic terms. The Santa Fe Trail, of course, was not traveled by pure romantics, but rather in the main by hard-headed businessmen—solid Yankee merchants out of Missouri, who were willing to risk life and fortune in a bold bid to transport salable merchandise across a storm-tossed, Indian-patrolled prairie ocean in hopes of realizing a profit in Mexico's provincial capital of Santa Fe. But though engagement in commerce was their primary motive, they were not immune to the exotic lure of the trail, as Marian Russell would later describe it.

Most of the rough-edged Missouri traders had never been out of their own country. To them distant New Mexico, with its different language, customs, architecture, and natural scenery exerted a special appeal quite apart from its attraction as a marketplace. To embark upon a summer season of

Teamsters pose at the end of the Santa Fe Trail. (Ben Wittick photo, Museum of New Mexico, negative no. 15817)

trading in Santa Fe and share the comradeship of other men similarly engaged, in a dangerous crossing of the plains, provided an opportunity for adventure that many were quick to seize. The theater of their activity was so vast, the action so memorable, and the backdrop of landscape so picturesque, that it is scarcely surprising that writers should attempt to celebrate it all in poetry.

The meaning of the shining vision of the far Southwest is caught in a single line of a poem dating from the early 1850s. The last verse reads:

> *Then hold your horses, Billy,*
> *Just hold them for a day;*

I've crossed the River Jordan,
And am bound for Santa Fe.[11]

The key line is the third one, with its reference to crossing
the River Jordan. Beyond that river lay the promised land, in
this case New Mexico. And at the end of the trail awaited
the New Jerusalem, or Santa Fe, with its sunlit plaza, where
merchants could hope to find their pot of gold at rainbow's
end. Here was the stuff of poetry, indeed!

So much so that more than one hundred years later, the
bards are still at work. In 1982 Welborn Hope, recognized
as Oklahoma's "tramp poet," published his 176-page *The
Prairie Ocean: An Epic Poem of the Santa Fe Trail*. In it he
caught the dreamlike quality of a caravan's arrival in the
promised land, as witnessed in these lines:

> *Through Pecos village soon we passed, and saw*
> *The far blue ranges of Sandia—now*
> *A vast plateau we traveled, taking us*
> *Due north to Santa Fe, our Rainbow's End.*
> *We saw the far-off wave-like mountains rise*
> *In billows as if beaten up by wind—*
> *Up from the Prairie Ocean's body heaved*
> *Eight hundred miles by an enormous gale.*
> *Sweet Santa Fe! Before us in late sun,*
> *A sweep of low carnelian-colored hills*
> *Ran red like muscled arms into the town.*[12]

The Santa Fe Trail thus remains the domain of the poet as well as the scholar. As long as some of its history is still untold and some of its poetic images are yet to be formed in words, the long old trail will continue to attract writers in search of their own literary promised land.

NOTES

1. Both the editorial comment and the poem can be found in *Westport Historical Quarterly* 7 (June 1971): 10–11.

2. David J. Weber, ed., *Albert Pike, Prose Sketches and Poems* (Albuquerque: Calvin Horn, 1967); and John E. Sunder, ed., *Matt Field on the Santa Fe Trail* (Norman: University of Oklahoma Press, 1960).

3. David K. Strate, *Sentinel to the Cimarron* (Dodge City: Cultural Heritage and Arts Center, 1970), 77–78.

4. The Bishop's quote and the poem are found in Anna C. Minogue, *Loretto, Annals of the Century* (New York: America Press, 1912), 144–46.

5. Paul Horgan, *Lamy of Santa Fe* (New York: Farrar, Straus and Giroux, 1975), 343, 349.

6. "Notes and Documents," *New Mexico Historical Review* 26 (1951): 152.

7. *Santa Fe Trail Magazine* 1 (September 1913): 2.

8. Quoted by Margaret Long, *The Santa Fe Trail* (Denver: W. H. Kistler, 1954), 3.

9. Katie Lee, *Ten Thousand Goddam Cattle* (Flagstaff: Northland Press, 1976), 221–22.

10. Mrs. Hal Russell, ed., *Land of Enchantment, Memoirs of Marian Russell on the Santa Fe Trail* (Evanston: Branding Iron Press, 1954), 71.

11. W. W. H. Davis, *El Gringo; or, New Mexico and Her People* (Santa Fe: Rydal Press, 1938), 4.

12. Welborn Hope, *The Prairie Ocean, An Epic Poem of the Santa Fe Trail* (Oklahoma City: Oklahoma Historical Society, 1982), 57.

COMETS AND METEORS
ON THE SANTA FE TRAIL

Travelers camping on western trails had the clear night sky for a ceiling, and that dark bowl could sometimes put on a spectacular display. Comets and meteors, regarded in that day as "remarkable astronomical events," inspired awe and fear among people lodged upon the open prairie. Those crossing the Santa Fe Trail not infrequently mentioned such celestial sightings in their diaries.

David Kellogg, camped on Cottonwood Creek in eastern Kansas, for example, wrote in his journal for September 26, 1858: "The comet has been very brilliant for the last two evenings; it stretches clear across the Western sky. . . . The night watch passes quickly by as we gaze at the flaming wonder in the heavens."[1] What he witnessed was Donati's comet, seen all over the United States and described as "a brilliant light with a prodigious tail curved like a scimitar."[2]

In the nineteenth century, not much was known about the origin and nature of comets. As in ages past, many people superstitiously believed that they radiated heat that affected the earth's temperature and caused changes in the climate. Others thought that comets were the source of epidemics. And the most widely held belief was that they were warnings or omens of impending disasters, brought on by human sins.[3]

During the era of the Santa Fe Trail, there were a number of prominent comets and an astonishing meteor shower visible to western travelers. Biela's comet, which returned every seven years, appeared in 1825, four years after Becknell opened the trail. When it came again in 1832, many citizens were terrified, because it was calculated to pass closer to earth than ever before. Halley's comet was observed in 1835. Upon Biela's return in 1839, it could not be observed, since it passed near the sun. Its last sighting was in 1846, an important year in trail history, when an astronomer through his telescope saw the comet split in two.[4] The appearance of comets and meteors were events widely reported in the frontier press.

The great comet of 1843, with its brilliant tail said to measure 123 million miles in length, was the most startling of all. First seen in the West on March 3 and visible even in the daytime, it came streaming toward earth on what many feared was a collision course. The Reverend William Miller preached that it was a divine sign foretelling the destruction of the world.[5] Trail chronicler Josiah Gregg charted the progress of this comet using a spyglass, sextant, and compass. He later published his mathematical observations in a border newspaper, the *Arkansas Intelligencer*. Therein he noted that "the ignorant and superstitious attributed the extraordinary cold sea-

Kiowa pictograph showing "winter the stars fell," 1833–34. (after James Mooney)

son we have had" to advent of the comet. And Gregg added: "The above class of people . . . believe that the comet and the weather are signs of the fulfillment of Miller's prophecy."[6] Curiously David Kellogg also mentions in his trail journal that Kiowas he met in western Kansas thought that comets brought cold weather in their wake.[7]

The most memorable of all celestial phenomena occurred on the night of November 12, 1833, with the Leonid meteor shower that lit up the sky in every corner of the country.[8]

Reconstructed Bent's Old Fort on the Mountain Branch of the trail. (author's photo)

The *American Journal of Science* described it thus: "The first appearance was that of fireworks of the most imposing grandeur, covering the entire vault of heaven with myriads of fire-balls resembling skyrockets."[9] Sixteen-year-old Richard Smith Elliott (who would march with General S. W. Kearny to the conquest of Santa Fe in 1846) viewed the spectacle while attending an apple-butter party on a Missouri farm. "Thousands of stars," he wrote, "were apparently darting towards the earth and more following. We were all badly scared. The world seemed doomed."[10]

Missourians of Independence, on the eastern end of the Santa Fe Trail, took fright, thinking that the shooting stars were a protest from heaven for their recent persecution of Mormons. At the far end of the trail, in Santa Fe, Mexican residents experienced panic as well. In between these two points, William Bent and other overland traders watched the meteor display from the adobe walls of the still unfinished Bent's Fort.[11]

Camped in the vicinity were Southern Cheyennes, the tribe from whence came William's Indian wife, Owl Woman. His half-Cheyenne son, George, would later say: "The great meteor shower arrived in November and all the Indians thought the world was coming to an end. The dogs collected in bands and howled like wolves, the women and children wailed, and the warriors mounted their war horses and rode about, singing their death songs."[12] Ever after in Cheyenne history, the event was referred to as "The Night the Stars Fell." Author David Lavender used that dramatic phrase as a chapter title in his classic trail book, *Bent's Fort*.

One other odd incident associated with this 1833 shower of meteors took place in central Missouri, near the head of the Santa Fe Trail. A group of farmers had kidnapped a free black man, whom they planned to sell to a Missouri River slave buyer for the sum of $1200. The party with its captive was at the landing waiting for a southbound steamboat when the downpour of meteors began. The woods and even the river itself appeared to be on fire. The farmers concluded that judgement day was at hand and they had been caught in the illegal business of "running South" a free black. They promptly tore off his chains and sent him on his way. In the light of a new day, with the planet still intact, the farmers began to regret their loss of $1200.

It is reported that the individual whom the meteor shower had liberated fled southwestward on the Santa Fe Trail, married a Mexican woman, and eventually became a wealthy man. If that was the case, he was probably the first black to travel the trail; it is unfortunate that his name has thus far not come to light.[13]

There are probably many other undiscovered stories about comets and meteors associated with trade and travel on the Santa Fe Trail. It would pay interested readers to keep a lookout for them.

NOTES

1. Quoted in Marc Simmons, ed., *On the Santa Fe Trail* (Lawrence: University Press of Kansas, 1986), 55.

2. R. M. Devens, *American Progress: Or the Great Events of the Greatest Century* (Topeka: Herbert S. Reed, 1890), 305.

3. "Comets," in *The Penny Magazine,* October 27, 1832.

4. Bernard DeVoto, *The Year of Decision, 1846* (Boston: Houghton Mifflin Co., 1961), 3–4.

5. Devens, *American Progress,* 300–301. There seem to have been two comets in 1843. The second, called Mauvais's comet, appeared later in the year; *Niles National Register,* August 12, 1843.

6. Maurice Garland Fulton, ed., *Diary & Letters of Josiah Gregg,* 2 vols. (Norman: University of Oklahoma Press, 1941), 1:124.

7. Simmons, *On the Santa Fe Trail,* 59.

8. Proceeding from the constellation Leo Major, the shower had been visible in 1799 and would come again in 1866.

9. Quoted in Richard Smith Elliott, *Notes Taken in Sixty Years* (St. Louis: R. P. Studley & Co., 1883), 49.

10. Elliott, *Notes Taken in Sixty Years,* 49.

11. David Lavender, *Bent's Fort* (Garden City, NY: Doubleday & Co., 1954) 140–41.

12. George E. Hyde, *Life of George Bent, Written from His Letters* (Norman: University of Oklahoma Press, 1968), 51.

13. Floyd C. Shoemaker, ed., *Missouri—Day by Day,* 2 vols. (Columbia: State Historical Society of Missouri, 1942–43) 2:350–51.

PART THREE

SKETCHES OF THE TRAIL

MASSACRE OF THE COLES

SOME YEARS AGO I happened to be in the public library at Boonville, Missouri, doing research on the Santa Fe Trail. Boonville sits on the south bank of the Missouri River, opposite the site of Old Franklin, which marked the start of the trail in the early 1820s.

A young man approached me and said the librarian had informed him I was from New Mexico. His hobby was history, and he had a question for me.

It seems that a Captain Stephen Cole and his young nephew, also named Stephen Cole, had gone to New Mexico to trade in 1822, that is, just one year after the opening of the Santa Fe Trail. They were members of a prominent Boonville pioneer family.

According to sketchy reports, both Coles had been killed by Indians somewhere along the Rio Grande. Had I ever heard of this incident, the young man wanted to know. And could I furnish him any further details.

The story was complete news to me, and I was surprised that it could have gotten by me. There were very few Americans in the far Southwest that early, and the killing of two of them, no doubt the first to be slain by Indians in New Mexico, should have been highly publicized.

So far as we know, three parties of traders went over the trail from Old Franklin in 1822, so the Coles must have accompanied one of them.

The first party was led by William Becknell, who is credited with having blazed the trail to Santa Fe the previous year. The second, composed of about fifteen men, was under Colonel Benjamin Cooper. And the third party had a man named John Heath at its head. For none of these groups is there a roster showing the names of participants.

On the Kansas plains, the Becknell and Heath parties appear to have joined forces and continued together to Santa Fe. Probably the two Coles were with them, since the Cooper men are known to have headed for Taos instead of the capital.

I told my questioner in Boonville that I would keep a lookout and try to turn up clues as to the fate of the pair of Stephen Coles. It has taken me almost ten years, but I have finally located a brief account in a frontier newspaper (*Missouri Intelligencer,* April 10, 1824) that tells of their deaths.

Once in Santa Fe, the captain and his nephew put together their own outfit and started alone down the Rio Grande. Their purpose and destination are unknown. But we can guess that they rode south to test the trade possibilities in El Paso and Chihuahua.

Within a few years, Americans would routinely follow the

Navajos (Charles M. Bell photo, Museum of New Mexico, negative no. 3250)

Chihuahua Trail to engage in commerce. But at this early date it was a new idea, so the Coles were pioneers.

After several days, they camped on the shore of the Rio Grande below Albuquerque. It was August, and a small village could be seen on the far side of the river.

That evening a Navajo war party, unseen, observed them from a nearby hill. The Indians assumed that the two men were Spaniards, with whom they were then at war.

In the middle of the night, the Navajos entered the camp and killed the Coles, evidently while they slept. Only upon examining the long rifles and other strange equipment did they realize their victims were Americans, not Spaniards. According to the newspaper account,

The mistake filled them with grief. They did not strip the Coles as they do with their enemies and left with them a part of their baggage.

Afterwards, in a conversation with an American gentleman, they described through an interpreter, their feelings of sorrow and regret which the error had occasioned them.

The Navajos explained that the few Americans they had seen always treated them kindly; that they were a good and brave nation, against whom they had no enmity; and that they were distressed at killing their friends, and as a result had ridden from the death scene mortified and displeased.

The newspaper ended its story of the incident with an editorial comment: "This attitude of the Navajos shows a nobleness of mind, a respect for our national character, and a strong attachment to the principles of justice."

On the Missouri frontier, word of the Coles' slaying was greeted with an outpouring of grief. Captain Cole was eulogized as a natural leader of men, and one who loved wild adventure. But that thirst for adventure had led to his untimely death.

II

AN OLD-TIMER RETURNS

IN THE SUMMER of 1883, the elderly Mr. Reuben Gentry of Kentucky paid a return visit to Santa Fe, after an absence of more than thirty years. A local newspaper, the *Daily New Mexican,* (September 1, 1883) thought his recollections of old days in the Southwest of sufficient interest to give them extensive coverage in its pages.

His interviewer described Gentry as "a well preserved gentleman in his 60s who retains a keen recall of the past and has a good faculty for relating what he knows." And he added that the visitor was much astonished by the many changes in the capital and by the fact that most of the people he had originally known were now dead.

A few familiar landmarks still remained, Gentry observed. The San Miguel Mission, La Fonda Hotel, and adobe Governors Palace were easily identified. But he almost failed to recognize a sprawling building on Burro Alley that in his day

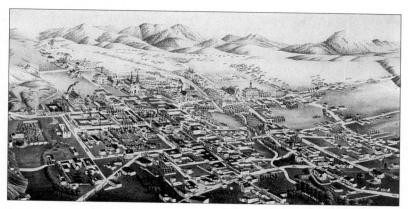

Santa Fe as it looked at the time of Reuben Gentry's visit. (Museum of New Mexico, negative no. 23306)

had housed the popular resort and gambling den of the notorious Doña Tules.

There Manuel Armijo, last Mexican governor of the territory, ran a monte bank. Now, however, it had been converted into the chambers of the district court and was occupied by the territorial chief justice.

As he told the journalist, Reuben Gentry had first come to Santa Fe in 1839, over the trail from Missouri. He was employed as supercargo (that is, wagonmaster) for a caravan of merchandise destined for New Mexico and Chihuahua.

This caravan numbered thirty wagons, each laden with 5 tons of dry goods, and supported by 250 oxen and mules and sixty employees. After paying the Mexican customs duty on the Santa Fe plaza, the train had continued on to Chihuahua City for final disposal of its wares.

The following year, Gentry had come out from Missouri again, a wagon trip that lasted forty days. This time he carried his own merchandise, with which he opened a store at Santa Fe.

In 1841 the famed Texas–Santa Fe Expedition from Austin invaded New Mexico. Governor Armijo managed to capture the whole party. Three of the Texan prisoners were lodged next to Gentry's store. He furnished them with supplies for an escape, but the trio was captured in flight and executed.

Two years later Reuben Gentry sold out his store and went to Mexico. At the city of Zacatecas, he was hired by an English mercantile firm to begin freighting goods overland from Independence, Missouri. These wares had been purchased in London and shipped to the American frontier, where they awaited transfer to Zacatecas.

For the next four years, Gentry prospered in this business. One of his employees during this period was James Magoffin (brother-in-law of Santa Fe Trail diarist Susan Magoffin), who later became prominent as an El Paso developer.

When the Mexican War broke out in 1846, Reuben Gentry happened to be in Independence, loading his wagons with British goods. Owing to the conflict, it appeared he would not be able to make his deliveries in Zacatecas. But by pulling strings, he was able to secure a British passport.

With that document as his security, he led his caravan to New Mexico, in the wake of a conquering U.S. Army. From Santa Fe he moved down the Rio Grande to Valverde, below

Socorro, where he had been instructed to wait for the troops of Colonel Alexander Doniphan.

When his teamsters became restive, Gentry decided to risk the journey south without the protection of soldiers. At El Paso he found the town "all in confusion with war preparations" and pushed on quickly to Chihuahua City.

There he was arrested by Mexican authorities. However, when he displayed his British passport and presented papers showing that he had English goods in transit, he was promptly released.

From that point on he had no more difficulties, safely delivering his cargo to its destination. That proved to be his last venture in Mexico.

Reflecting on those palmy days, Gentry told the journalist in 1883 that average profits in the Santa Fe trade had amounted to 200 percent on imported dry goods. No other frontier business, he noted, offered such a rich reward.

The newspaper story informed readers that after an overnight stay in Santa Fe, Mr. Gentry had departed by rail for El Paso and Chihuahua.

"He will now make the entire trip from Kansas City to Chihuahua City in less than six days, where it used to require three months to cover the same distance when he passed over this exact route by oxen just 37 years ago."

═══≪≪≪≪≪ 12 ≫≫≫≫≫═══

HISTORIC COLD SPRINGS

ONE OF THE least known and seldom visited historic sites on the old Santa Fe Trail is Cold Springs. It is located on the edge of the Cimarron Valley, a few miles northwest of Boise City in the Oklahoma Panhandle.

A century and a half ago, when the great white-topped freight caravans from Missouri passed by, on their rumbling way to Santa Fe, Cold Springs served travelers as a welcome and friendly oasis.

Its bountiful supply of fresh water and a scattering of shade trees made a good campsite. And nearby rocky bluffs offered a handy place for people to carve their names and the date, as a record of their passing.

Some of the inscriptions still to be seen go back to the 1840s. Unfortunately many others were lost when the sandstone was quarried for building blocks. In 1960 the Oklahoma Historical Society made a complete record of the names that remain.

West of Cold Springs, the trail climbed onto a plain that tilted upward toward the distant Rabbit Ears Peaks, one of the best known landmarks along the road to Santa Fe. Even now, more than a hundred years after the last wagon train passed by, deeply incised trail ruts can be found in the vicinity of the springs.

The site had long been a favorite stopping place for roving Indians, both because of the water and the game trails that converged there. Unhappily for travelers, it also proved to be a prime ambush point. War parties lay in wait for merchant trains and later for stagecoaches carrying the U.S. mail. During the Civil War years, when the Indian danger was at its height, military patrols kept watch over Cold Springs to discourage villainy.

One prominent visitor to the springs was New Mexico Governor Manuel Armijo, who camped there with a force of five hundred men in June of 1843. He had marched out from Santa Fe several weeks before, intending to go all the way to the Arkansas River in western Kansas, which then marked the boundary between the United States and Mexico.

His purpose was to meet the spring merchant caravan from Missouri and guard it through hostile Indian country. A rumor was also circulating that the Republic of Texas had commissioned Colonel Jacob Snively to lead a band of adventurers northward and attack any New Mexicans found traveling the Santa Fe Trail.

With an army of five hundred at his back—regular soldiers of the Mexican army, citizens' militia, and Pueblo Indians— Governor Armijo believed he could handle any trouble that

Governor Manuel Armijo, who led the expedition to Cold Spring in 1843.
(Museum of New Mexico, negative no. 50809)

might arise. Mounted on a gray mule, which he customarily rode on campaigns, the governor wore a flashy uniform and a tall hat topped by a graceful plume.

It is known that Armijo invested heavily in the Santa Fe trade, so it seems likely the approaching caravan carried some of his own goods, purchased by his agents in Independence and St. Louis. That could explain why he had taken personal command of what, otherwise, was a fairly routine escort mission.

The outcome, however, proved anything but routine. At Cold Springs Armijo called a halt. For some reason he decided to stop there and send an advance party under Captain Ventura Lovato on to the Arkansas River. Perhaps with the approach of mid-June, the weather had turned hot and the governor decided that resting in cottonwood shade by cool water was preferable to dry marches.

In any case Captain Lovato cut out one hundred men, many of them Indians from Taos Pueblo, and left Cold Springs to meet the wagons. He rode some 140 miles to a stretch of low sandhills below the Arkansas. There he ran straight into an ambush set by Colonel Snively.

The New Mexicans, outnumbered two to one, fought gamely. But after eighteen of them were killed and many more wounded, they surrendered. A couple of the men got away in the confusion and rushed back to Cold Springs with word of the disaster.

In their fright, they reported that Snively's Texans numbered in the hundreds. That news turned Armijo's camp into

Cold Spring, on the Cimarron Cutoff in the Oklahoma Panhandle. Today the spring is enclosed in the open stone building at right. Travelers carved their names on the rocks located between the trees at upper left. (author's photo)

bedlam. Without waiting for orders, segments of his army broke up and rushed to take the trail back to Santa Fe.

A few days later, the merchant train reached Cold Springs, having gotten safely by both Indians and Texans. Strewn about was all kinds of equipment, including spurs, bridles, and lariats, cast aside by Armijo's troops in the hurly-burly of their departure. Without further incident, the wagons went on to Santa Fe.

The Pueblo Indians had suffered the most casualties in the battle with Snively. From that day forward, they nursed a grudge against Texans and Americans both.

Three and a half years later, the people of Taos Pueblo re-belled and massacred several foreigners, including the first American governor, Charles Bent. He was a noted Santa Fe trader and the builder of Bents Fort in southeastern Colorado. At the time it was reported that the Indians were seeking blind revenge for their losses in the old battle east of Cold Springs.

Governor Manuel Armijo had merely lost some of his equipment at the springs. But in the late 1860s, another New Mexican party that stopped there left behind a cluster of graves.

An ox train owned by José Perea of Bernalillo, New Mex-ico, was returning from Kansas City. As the wagons skirted the Cimarron River, cholera broke out. Teamsters dropped in their tracks and were placed in the vehicles, until barely enough were left standing to handle the oxen.

At Cold Springs the wagon boss called a halt. A case of Penguin whiskey was broken open and mixed with New Mexico red chile. That was the standard treatment for the dread cholera.

But the remedy failed to help. Twelve days later, when the wagons finally said good-by to Cold Springs, fresh mounds of earth marked the last resting place of men who would never see their families again.

13

LANDMARKS OF THE PIONEERS

I DROVE PAST the Wagon Mound the other day, one of my favorite landmarks in eastern New Mexico. The low mountain forms a nearly perfect profile of a covered wagon drawn by a team of oxen.

A century ago travelers entering the territory got their first glimpse of the mound from the summit of Raton Pass, eighty miles away. They could also see a smaller, round hill immediately to the north, Pilot Knob. The distant trail to Santa Fe, as they well knew, led through a narrow pass between the knob and the Wagon Mound.

Interstate 25 today follows the identical route. But since the name Pilot Knob no longer occurs on road maps, I feel sure that not one of the thousands of motorists who speed by each year knows the hill's identity or is aware of its former significance as a major beacon guiding the course of caravans.

In the days when all travel was by horse, mule, or ox power, landmarks named Pilot Knob were fairly common on western trails. I know of at least two others in the Southwest.

Marble grave marker for a Santa Fe Trail freighter in the Wagon Mound Cemetery. (author's collection)

One lies on the edge of the lower Colorado River, astride the trail running from El Paso across southern New Mexico and Arizona to San Diego.

The other Pilot Knob is in extreme northeastern New Mexico, not far from the border with Oklahoma. Today it is known as Rabbit Ears Peak.

Actually Spanish explorers first called it Rabbit Ears, and that is what it was until the 1820s or so, when freighters from Missouri, using it to steer by far out on the plains, changed the name to Pilot Knob. But when the era of the wagon trains was over, settlers in the area went back to using Rabbit Ears. Perhaps they liked the sound better.

It is easy to see how the landmark got its name. The peak is really two peaks, closely aligned, which from a distance appear for all the world like a pair of ears topping a rabbit's head.

Former State Senator William Wheatley of Clayton, who knows his local history, tells me there is another explanation for the name. Spaniards fought a battle there in the eighteenth century against a large war party of hostile Cheyenne, he says. The soldiers were victorious and killed the chief and many warriors. The chief's name was Rabbit Ears!

Like Pilot Knob, the phrase "Point of Rocks" was a common designation on early day trails. Any rocky bluff, such as the tip of a mesa, that forced wagons to swing wide around its base was apt to be graced with the title. There were no fewer than three on the Santa Fe Trail—two in Kansas and one in New Mexico, a few miles east of Springer. Another Point of Rocks was located at the southern end of the Jor-

The Pilot Knob, a major trail landmark just north of the Wagon Mound. (photo by Evelyn Vinogradov)

nada del Muerto, above Las Cruces on the El Paso–Santa Fe road.

Still a third type of landmark familiar to pioneer caravans was the inscription or autograph rock, a place where faces of smooth stone invited passers-by to carve their name and the date.

Independence Rock on the Oregon Trail in Wyoming and Pawnee Rock on the Santa Fe Trail in central Kansas were popular locations for leaving inscriptions. So too was the Hueco Tanks, a rocky spot 35 miles east of El Paso, where the Butterfield Company maintained a stagecoach station in the 1850s.

But the best known and the most significant, in the Southwest at least, is the celebrated Inscription Rock, now El Morro National Monument. It is situated on an old Spanish trail that ran from the Rio Grande Valley and Acoma Pueblo westward to Zuni. For more than 350 years, Europeans have been leaving a record of their passing. Juan de Oñate, New Mexico's founder and first governor, was one of the earliest to sign. His inscription begins, "Pasó por aquí," that is, "He passed by here"; and then, "Commander Don Juan de Oñate from the discovery of the South Sea on April 16, 1605." On that date the governor was returning to the Rio Grande Valley after an overland march to the Gulf of California, which he called the South Sea.

If Oñate's phrase has a familiar ring, the reason is that Eugene Manlove Rhodes used it as the title of his most famous novel, set in southern New Mexico and first published in 1926.

Names of many other Spaniards, known and little-known, can be found carved at El Morro, among them the reconquerer Diego de Vargas (1692) and Bishop Elizaecochea of Durango, Mexico (1737). Later the first archbishop of New Mexico, the Frenchman Jean B. Lamy, cut his signature there, in the year 1863.

Writer Charles F. Lummis once described this place as "the Stone Autograph Album." Such "albums," wherever they occur in the West, are a reminder that people in the past, just as today, had a strong desire to be remembered by history, even for so simple a thing as incising their name in rock on a public register.

14

OXEN VERSUS MULES

I N T H E D A Y S of the Old West, wagon freighters often sat around the campfire arguing the merits of oxen versus mules, the way men today will argue the advantages of one brand of car or truck over another. Serious things that pertain to the open road, it seems, have always engaged masculine attention.

The oxen vs. mules debate was not easily settled. Teamsters accustomed to driving a yoke of oxen would swear by their draft animals and claim that the mule was an inferior beast. Mule skinners, on the other hand, were just as convinced that their animals were perfect for long-distance hauling and that the dumb ox could not compete.

In truth the ox and the mule each had his selling points, his special qualifications that made him useful at pulling a three-thousand-pound freight wagon loaded to the top of its sideboards. But both also had unique disadvantages that worked against them.

One of the earliest writers to treat the matter was Josiah

Gregg, in his classic *Commerce of the Prairies,* published in 1844. He said that oxen could pull heavier loads than the same number of mules, especially through muddy or sandy places. But they did not have the same endurance and fell off rapidly in weight. At the end of a thousand-mile trip, mules still looked good, but oxen would be poor and might have to be sold for as little as $10 a yoke.

Captain Randolph B. Marcy, who wrote a handy guide in 1859 called *The Prairie Traveler: A Handbook for Overland Expeditions,* expressed a preference for mules. They moved faster and withstood the heat of summer much better than oxen. But Marcy had to admit that oxen were more economical to acquire. At frontier towns oxen cost about $25, as compared to mules, which sold for $100 apiece. At that price the freighter could afford to take along more spare oxen as replacements.

Marcy's reference to mules standing up to heat was true. They could work long hours in the hot sun because, like other equines, they perspired and thereby cooled off. Their sweat glands acted as a sort of thermostat. Work oxen, by contrast, lacked those glands and so had to stop when overheated and seek shade. Bullwhackers, as ox drovers were known, were aware of that, so they started at dawn, drove til the heat rose, stopped during midday, and then continued for a few hours in the late afternoon and evening.

Another aspect of the discussion had to do with the performance of oxen and mules during Indian raids. Gregg thought that mules, being nervous animals, were quicker to run at the first shot. But oxen, he declared, were the worst once they

Modern oxen yoked to a freight wagon on the Santa Fe Trail in Missouri. (photo courtesy Denny Davis)

got started on a stampede, simply because they were so difficult to stop.

Old-time plainsmen had a soft spot for mules, because they were said to be able to smell approaching Indians. On night guard they would watch a mule's ears; if they started to twitch vigorously, it was a safe bet that warriors were creeping up on the wagon train.

It was an accepted fact that Indians would attack a freight caravan to steal the mules, which they used for riding and packing. But they would never stage a raid to acquire oxen, since they had no use for those animals, the buffalo providing them all the meat they needed.

Both the ox and the mule had hard, flinty feet, and on the

sandy plains neither generally needed to be shod. Indeed the bottom of the hoofs wore smooth, and on dry grassy surfaces they sometimes slipped as if they were walking on ice. Rocky country, however, was another matter. Then a draft animal needed iron shoes to prevent sore feet. Mules, even if balky, presented little problem. A stout man could pick up a foot and nail on a shoe anywhere along the trail.

But you cannot do that with an ox, because he is unable to stand on three legs. Therefore blacksmith shops on the border customarily had a set of stocks, a wooden mechanical device that clamped onto the ox and turned him on his side, so that the smith could attach a set of shoes.

What was to be done, however, if oxen required shoeing on the road with no stocks available? Occasionally a narrow trench was dug and the animal, with the aid of ropes, was spilled into that on his back. At other times rawhide shoes, like moccasins, were slipped on the oxen's feet for temporary use.

The one point over which there existed no dispute had to do with the temperment of each animal. Everyone acknowledged that the mule was cantankerous and unlovable, while the ox showed the qualities of a household pet.

The bullwhacker always mourned the loss of an ox. But no teamster, so far as the record goes, ever mourned for a mule.

15

CHILDHOOD MEMORIES
OF TERESINA BENT

Today in New Mexico few people remember the name of Teresina Bent. But in her time she was an eye-witness to one of the tragedies of our history—the assassination of her father, Charles Bent, the first American governor of New Mexico.

As a mature lady living in the twentieth century, Teresina dictated her recollection* of the event, which had occurred at the Bent home in Taos on January 19, 1847, when she was but five years old. No doubt her account included details picked up later from her mother, Maria Ignacia Jaramillo.

Famed Santa Fe trader Charles Bent had been given the governorship the year before by General Stephen W. Kearny. That followed upon the conquest and occupation of New Mexico at the outbreak of the Mexican War.

After presiding for several months in Santa Fe, the gover-

*On file, Kit Carson Historic Museum, Taos.

nor decided to visit his family at Taos. The army advised him that some of the native people, resentful of the occupation, were threatening a revolt. Bent, however, said the Taos residents were his friends and he entertained no fear for his safety.

Teresina relates that the attack against her father came about six in the morning. A mob of local citizens and Indians from nearby Taos Pueblo gathered in front of the house and set up a howl. The terrified family, still in night clothes, barred the front door. One of the Indian leaders shouted that they had come to kill the governor. And as Teresina remembers it, he added: "No American is going to govern us!"

As some of the mob began to chop at the door with hatchets, Mrs. Bent urged her husband to escape out the back, seize one of the horses in the corral, and flee. He replied: "It would not do for a governor to run away and leave his loved ones in danger. If they want to kill me, they can kill me here with my family."

And that is exactly what happened! The assailants broke through the door and shot the governor full of arrows before the horrified eyes of his kin. While he still breathed, one of them scalped him with a bow string.

Teresina says that her mother would have been slain, too, but a faithful servant shielded her from the arrows, dying in the noble effort. Finally some cooler heads in the mob got Bent's suvivors out a side door and into hiding.

Shortly thereafter the American army arrived and stormed Taos Pueblo, defeating the rebels. A vivid memory Teresina carried to her grave was a picture of six ringleaders hanging by their necks in the center of the Taos plaza.

After Teresina was left fatherless, she and her mother went with relatives to settle in Rayado, across the mountains to the east, at the edge of the plains. It was a dangerous place, subject to frequent attacks by nomadic tribes. Once when most of the men were away, a large war party of Cheyennes appeared. They demanded food. It was thought best to comply, but at the same time a messenger was sent secretly to Fort Union with an urgent plea for help.

All the women set to work cooking—meat, coffee, whatever was available. Looking back on this traumatic incident, Teresina wrote: "I was 12 years old and the chief saw me and wanted to buy me to make me his wife.

"He kept offering horses—10, 15, 20 horses. We were all told not to make the chief angry. My, I was so frightened!

"While I carried platters of food from the kitchen, the tears were running down my cheeks. That made the chief laugh. He was bound to buy me, and when they all got through eating he said they would camp in front of our house. If I was not delivered by sundown, he would take me by force."

The women were greatly alarmed. They began assembling guns and bullets in preparation for a fight. They feared they might even have to withstand a siege.

As the sun dropped behind the western ridge of mountains, the Indians began to stir. The time was up and the Cheyennes were making preparations to spirit little Teresina away. One can imagine the terror of a child in those circumstances. Then suddenly at the last moment, in a scene reminiscent of a latter-day Hollywood movie, a trumpet

Teresina Bent, daughter of Governor Charles Bent. (New Mexico State Records Center photo)

sounded in the distance. A company of soldiers from Fort Union came galloping up the valley. The Indians hastily decamped and little Teresina was saved.

She wrote: "Then I cried and cried some more. I was so glad to see the soldiers. I did not want to go with the dirty chief."

In 1854 Teresina married a German immigrant, Aloys Scheurich. She spent her last years in Clovis, New Mexico, where she died in 1920.

Not long ago in a used bookstore, I found a copy of *The Bent Family in America*. It had belonged to Teresina. Her name was written on the flyleaf.

How delighted I was to own a book that this gallant pioneer lady had once held in her hands and read. It is one of the chief treasures in my personal library.

16

NEW MEXICO'S ITALIAN HERMIT

O<small>F ALL THE</small> strange and colorful characters who have marched across the pages of New Mexico's history, there are few whose story can equal that of the hermit Juan Maria de Agostini. By the time he was murdered in the Organ Mountains east of Las Cruces in 1869, he had already carved a name for himself in the hearts of the pious folk along the Rio Grande.

Agostini's early history is obscure, but these details we know. He left his native Italy about the age of thirty to take up the life of a pilgrim and religious seeker. For five years he wandered around Spain visiting holy shrines, and then in 1838 he took ship for Venezuela. Over the next two decades, his wanderings by foot carried him to the remotest parts of South America. Much of this time he spent living in caves, but often he entered rural villages, where he would preach to the peasants and perform cures using various herbal formulas.

The hermit, Juan Maria de Agostine (Museum of New Mexico, negative no. 93160)

One side of his nature always seemed to be pulling him toward a life of solitude, but another made him restless and kept him constantly on the move. Through Central America, Mexico, and Cuba his travels led. Finally he decided to go to Canada, believing that there he would find a promised land and answers to his questions about the mystery of life. But Canada proved a disappointment—people were not receptive to long-bearded hermits, and the cold climate made living in caves disagreeable. There he had a vision instructing him to go West.

Agostini next appeared in Council Grove, Kansas, at the head of the Santa Fe Trail. By good fortune he fell in with Don Manuel Romero, a prominent New Mexican merchant, who was preparing to leave for his home in Las Vegas. Don Manuel was heading a large ox train, and he invited the odd-looking pilgrim to accompany him. Agostini agreed, but he refused a seat in the wagons. In spite of his sixty-two years, he walked the entire distance to New Mexico.

The Hispanic folk of Las Vegas took the wanderer to their hearts. They came to him in droves, asking advice and seeking cures. Many believed him to be a miracle worker, though he always disavowed that title. Leaders of the community offered him hospitality in their grand houses, but the Italian hermit preferred to sleep outside on the ground and to dine entirely on cornmeal mush.

The attention he was getting finally proved too much, and he moved up to the top of the Cerro de Tecolote (Owl Mountain), eighteen miles east of Las Vegas. There was even a convenient cave to serve as home. But his devoted follow-

Hermit's Peak loomed on the horizon as wagons approached Las Vegas, New Mexico, on the Santa Fe Trail. (Museum of New Mexico, negative no. 119852)

ers would not give him the solitude he craved. Weather permitting, they filed up the steep trail to bring their problems to him. Some of them, deciding that a cave was no place for a holy man, built him a small log cabin.

For five years the aging recluse stuck to his mountaintop, while his fame spread among the villages in the surrounding country. Then he announced he was leaving to pick up his long journey again.

In the spring of 1867, he appeared in the town of Mesilla. As before he gave counsel and prescribed remedies for the sick. Colonel Albert Fountain befriended him and offered him the shelter of his home. But Agostini was a hermit through and through. A cave was what he wanted, and he found one high in the Organ Mountains overlooking the Mesilla Valley.

One day in April 1869, Colonel Fountain took some men and went to the mountains to check on his friend. They discovered to their horror that the kindly pilgrim had been murdered. He was lying on the ground with a dagger between his shoulder blades, as if he had been slain while kneeling at prayer. Who could have performed such a terrible and senseless deed? The mystery was never solved.

Today certain folk in the vicinity of Las Vegas make yearly pilgrimages to the top of the mountain where Juan Maria de Agostini once lived and taught. They plant small wooden crosses near the ruins of his cabin. The mountain is no longer called the Cerro de Tecolote. For a hundred years it has been known as Hermit's Peak.

17

A PRIMER ON MATCHES

WITH SMOKING ON the wane and much of home heating operating on automatic pilot, I have noticed there is less demand for matches than there was even a few years ago. Nonetheless the match remains a rather basic item, one we often take for granted.

When was the match first introduced in New Mexico? That is a question I have been trying to answer for some time, without much success.

One possible clue is provided by a little incident that occurred in Fayette, Missouri, during the summer of 1829. John C. McCoy, one of the founders of Kansas City, related it at an old-timers' convention in 1880.*

He recalled that at eighteen he had been standing in front of the Fayette Hotel, when a merchant from nearby Boonville put a cigar in his mouth.

---

*Anonymous, *The History of Jackson County Missouri* (Kansas City: Union Historical Company, 1881), 157.

"Then he took from his pocket," continued McCoy, "something, the like of which I had never before seen, and few, if any others had ever seen west of the Mississippi. He rubbed it on the sole of his boot, and lo! there was combustion fire.

"It was the friction match, a new invention. Previous to that our only way to produce fire was with the cumbersome flint and steel."

Actually matches had been around since the late 1600s, when an Englishman, Robert Boyle, took small pieces of wood (known as splints) and dipped them in melted sulphur. These early examples were not very practical, though. To light the match, you had to dip the end in a small vial of sulphuric acid carried in the pocket.

This problem was solved more than a century later, it is said, by a French high school student who added phosphorus to the match tip. That allowed striking of the match on any rough surface. A few histories claim that an English chemist, John Walker, rather than the French student made this discovery in 1826. In any case within a short time, Walker was manufacturing and selling these friction matches at a mere halfpenny a box. They were quickly shipped abroad.

It was probably one of Walker's matches that John McCoy saw the Boonville merchant use. The significance of this is that Boonville was one of the starting points for the newly opened Santa Fe Trail. So anytime after 1829, somebody could have carried the first match over the long miles to New Mexico.

In 1864 a wholesale grocer in Leavenworth, Kansas, filled

an order for New Mexican merchant José Albino Baca and shipped it to him in Las Vegas, by way of the Santa Fe Trail. I have a copy of the invoice, and one of the entries listed is a box of matches at 75¢. The high cost of transportation by covered freight wagon made them expensive, indeed a luxury item. That is the first documented reference to matches I have seen, but I fully expect earlier mentions to turn up sooner or later. Of course they should date from after 1829.

With the advent of the railroad, I suspect matches imported from the East became cheaper, and hence more plentiful. Common brands of the day, in colorful boxes, were Elephant, Runaway, Pearl, and Tiger. Poor rural New Mexicans, nevertheless, kept using the old flint and steel into the opening years of the twentieth century.

In the late 1800s, cheap matches were made and widely sold to miners and ranchers. They were produced in blocks, with the heads stuck together, and packed for shipping in blue tin cans. When a match was needed, you broke one off from the block. The large amount of yellow sulphur and red phosphorus gave off a cloud of noxious fumes, with the odor of brimstone.

For that reason such matches were usually called "Lucifers." Agnes Morley Cleaveland, who grew up on a ranch in Socorro County, recalls that in cow country lingo, they had another name.

She wrote: "We tried to make life as tolerable as possible for the cowboys. They sometimes referred to ours as 'the ranch of the popping matches.'

"That was because we supplied them with the present

type of tipped match instead of the blocks of sulphur-headed matches whose fumes suggested the local name for them, 'hell-sticks.' Those matches would choke a cowboy to death before he got his cigarette lighted.

"Most ranches supplied 'hell-sticks.' But not us!"*

---

*No Life for a Lady (Boston: Houghton Mifflin, 1941), 160.

18

A TEENAGER'S ADVENTURES
ON THE FRONTIER

IN THE SUMMER of 1846, a seventeen-year-old Cincinnati resident, Lewis H. Garrard, started on a ten-month adventure that would take him to the far Southwest and back. Inspired by a reading of Fremont's account of Rocky Mountain explorations, he decided to see the frontier for himself.

"My parents were persuaded to let me go," Garrard wrote afterward. "And, they furnished me cash, a pocket Bible, a rifle, and a few calico shirts."* They also bought him a ticket on a steamer headed downriver to St. Louis.

In that city he took a room in the famed Planter's House and began looking for means to go West. By chance he made the acquaintance of Ceran St. Vrain, member of the firm of Bent, St. Vrain & Co., Indian and Mexican traders on the Santa Fe Trail.

Mr. St. Vrain was preparing to lead a freight caravan over

---

*All quotes are drawn from Garrard's *Wah-to-yah and the Taos Trail* (Norman: University of Oklahoma Press, 1955).

The young Lewis H. Garrard, soon after his New Mexico adventure. (after Blanche Grant)

the trail to Bent's Fort, in present-day southeastern Colorado. He invited Garrard to accompany him, and the eager youth jumped at the chance.

The slow trip across the vast and open plains filled the novice traveler with wonder. "The heat glimmering up from the parched ground dazzled the eye, and we rode as if on the ocean." After a trip that included buffalo chases and Indian encounters, Garrard and the caravan reached the fort, where he was introduced to the proprietor, William Bent. "We sat down to a table, for the first time in 50 days, and ate with knives, forks and plates."

The curious newcomer found the huge adobe-walled fort thronged with "a mixture of traders, government officers, hunters, Indians, Frenchmen, and New Mexicans." It was a scene to stir a young man in quest of adventure.

Rising early the morning after his arrival, Garrard climbed to the upper walls and took in a view of the Spanish Peaks, 120 miles to the west. The twin mountains were called the Wah-to-yah by the Utes, meaning in their language, "The Breasts of the World."

Over the next several weeks, young Garrard observed life in the fort and made prolonged visits to the tepee camps of the then friendly Cheyenne Indians, living nearby. William Bent was married to a Cheyenne woman, so whites were welcome among them.

Then in late January 1847, a mountain man brought startling news. Charles Bent, William's older brother, had been killed along with twenty others, in an uprising at Taos. Since the American conquest of New Mexico the previous year,

An interior view of Bent's Old Fort, as it might have appeared to Lewis H. Garrard. (author's photo)

Charles had served as civil governor. Garrard at once hurried to the fort, where all was hubbub. "We were apprehensive for our own safety," he relates, "for it was probable the country from El Paso to Taos had revolted, and a Mexican expedition might be expected to attack Bent's Fort." When that proved not to be the case, William enlisted twenty-three

The Spanish Peaks, a celebrated trail landmark in southeastern Colorado. (after Fremont)

volunteers, including Garrard, and rode down past the Spanish Peaks into New Mexico. Approaching Taos the company discovered that U.S. troops from Santa Fe had already captured the town.

Garrard was on hand to view the trial, conviction, and hanging of the rebel leaders. Apart from the official reports, he left us the only eye-witness account of those tragic events. Back at Bent's Fort by early spring, the boy decided he had seen enough of adventuring in the Wild West. Joining a military caravan, he found his way back to Missouri, and within weeks he was at home again in Cincinnati.

During his travels, Garrard kept notes of his experiences— "scanty pencilings," he called them. These he reworked and before his twentieth birthday published a book called *Wah-to-yah and the Taos Trail*. The subtitle read: *Or Prairie Travel and Scalp Dances, with a Look at Los Rancheros from Muleback and the Rocky Mountain Campfire*. For a time the book sold well, then went out of print. It was not reprinted until the twentieth century, when it was finally recognized as a major historical source on the Southwest.

Garrard's later life was unglamorous, even boring. He died at fifty-eight, his only enduring work having been performed while he was still in his teens.

Author and critic Bernard De Voto once declared, "Garrard's book is one of the best ever written about the West. It is an unacknowledged classic of our literature."

19

WHEN STAGECOACHES
RULED THE TRAIL

On my drives over the Santa Fe Trail to Missouri, I make a point of searching for the ruins of original stage stations. Although overlooked by many people, they form some of the most interesting historical remains to be seen today along the old trail.

Stagecoaching came late to New Mexico. Under the rule of Spain and Mexico, no public coaches ever ascended the Chihuahua Trail to El Paso, Albuquerque, and points north. Nor did any stages ply the Santa Fe Trail during the first quarter century of its existence. Not until 1850 did the first stagecoach set out from Independence for New Mexico.

A Missouri newspaper tells us about the new service. "The stages are got up in elegant style, and are each arranged to convey eight passengers. The bodies are beautifully painted, and made water-tight, with a view of using them as boats in ferrying streams. The team consists of six mules to each coach.

A stagecoach on the plains east of Las Vegas, New Mexico. (author's collection)

The mail is guarded by eight men, who with their many repeating arms are equal to a small army."

At first the stages departed once a month. Then later service became weekly and finally in the 1860s, daily. Fare for the two-week trip to Santa Fe was $250, with baggage limited to 40 pounds per passenger. Meals at the primitive stations were extra.

At Santa Fe through passengers could take another coach south to Mesilla and El Paso. There connections could be made with the San Antonio and San Diego Mail Line and later with its successor, the Butterfield Overland Mail coaches.

By all accounts a prolonged ride on those early-day stages was an experience not to be envied. Colonel Henry Inman,

Pigeon's Ranch, stage stop near the summit of Glorieta Pass, on the trail 15 miles east of Santa Fe. (Museum of New Mexico, negative no. 76032)

who knew about the matter firsthand, tells us that it was terribly crowded and uncomfortable, with no chance to stretch your limbs save for brief station stops. During blizzards passengers turned blue, and if Indians attacked, they might lose their hair and lives.

Fatigue was worst the first few days on the road. You sat bolt upright through the night, snatching winks between jostlings. But Inman says that after a while you got used to it, and the last part of the ride might be relatively comfortable.

Travel conditions on the Santa Fe Trail improved a bit during the later 1860s, with the building of more stations at intervals varying from 10 to 15 miles. But the food remained poor, the biscuits hard as cannonballs and the coffee a vile decoction, according to one description.

When you visit the few remaining stage stations today, strung along the trail, it is easy to imagine the lathered horses dashing up, the vehicle creaking to a halt, and the benumbed passengers staggering out. We are reminded that the romance of the old days was not all it has been cracked up to be.

One of the best preserved ruins at the eastern end of the trail is the McGee-Harris Stage Station, 4 miles from Scranton, Kansas. It is a rock and frame building, still roofed, sitting in a farmer's field at the crossing of 110 Mile Creek. Once a store and blacksmith shop stood nearby, but they have disappeared, their foundations plowed under.

Another station I like is a fine two-story adobe near Las Animas, Colorado, on the mountain branch of the Santa Fe Trail. It was also the home of J. W. Prowers, a local pioneer and friend of Kit Carson. Today it has been restored and is accessible to visitors.

A little farther west, about midway between La Junta and Trinidad, Colorado, are the remains of the Iron Springs Stage Station, built by the Missouri Stage Company in 1861. After several previous failures, I finally found the site on my last trail trip. There is not much to see; the stone foundation of the barn, built to repel Indian attack; a low mound where the adobe station once stood; and the stubs of posts buried in the ground marking the original corral. But the surrounding country of plains and mesas is virtually unchanged.

Perhaps the finest station yet standing in New Mexico is the Sapello Stage Station, on the west side of Watrous, about 15 miles east of Las Vegas. Bold ruts left by freight wagons and coaches lead right up to the front of the building. The rock structure with a pitched roof shows some modern improvements, but its historical integrity has been little impaired. Its current resident is an old-timer with the unlikely name of John Wayne.

Visiting these old stage stations helps call to mind the pioneering days, when life was hard yet full of zest and adventure. But for me, reading about fatigue and frost-bitten limbs is enough. I am not eager to experience them.

===≪≪≪≪≪ 20 ≫≫≫≫≫===

THE TRAIL'S OTHER SIDE

VISUALIZING WHAT IT was like to make a journey over the Santa Fe Trail, we inevitably form a picture of a wagon train assembling at Franklin, Independence, or Westport and striking out in a southwestward direction for the markets of Santa Fe and other cities below it. For details of such enterprises, our reliance is upon dozens of diaries and journals kept by Anglo American men, and a few women, who made the dangerous excursion to New Mexico.

What history books often neglect to tell us is that many Hispanos made the same trip, but in the opposite direction. Very early in the game, members of New Mexico's aristocratic families, such as the Oteros, Chavezes, Armijos, and Pereas, outfitted large caravans and sent them east filled with buffalo robes, blankets, and raw wool. Returning they brought back all kinds of manufactured goods, even heavy pieces of furniture. Those Hispano traders and their native wagon crews almost never kept personal journals, so their contribution to the trail's history has been all but forgotten.

Not long ago I came upon an unpublished manuscript—not really a diary, but the later recollections—of a New Mexican named José Gurulé, who went over the trail from Bernalillo to Kansas City in 1867, when he was sixteen years old. Mr. Gurulé set down his experiences in 1940, at the age of eighty-eight. His memory was still sharp, and his account probably represents the only one we have from the hand of a *peón,* that is from a man who went East not as an owner or wagon boss, but as a lowly drover. His brief document, therefore, is a valuable historical record.*

José Gurulé grew up in the tiny hamlet of Las Placitas, at the north end of the Sandia Mountains and a few miles east of Bernalillo. The *patrón,* or political boss, of that region was the great sheep baron and merchant prince, Don José Leandro Perea. He owned a huge hacienda on the banks of the Rio Grande and ran flocks of sheep numbering in the thousands. Practically all the local people, including the entire population of Las Placitas, were bound to Perea by a system of debt peonage; he advanced them money and they did his bidding whenever he called.

Each spring Perea loaded ten wagons with sacks of wool and sent them to Kansas City under his trusted wagon master, Esquipulo Romero. In preparation for the trip, Romero went to Las Placitas, lined up all the men in the plaza, and chose those he needed as helpers. He always picked men

---

*Gurulé Typescript, WPA File, Museum of New Mexico, Santa Fe.

José Leandro Perea of Bernalillo, New Mexico, owner of the wagons with which José Gurulé traveled to Kansas City. (Museum of New Mexico, negative no. 50560)

with strength and endurance. Thus it was that the teenager José Gurulé was tagged in 1867.

The Perea train rumbled eastward to Las Vegas on the edge of the plains, which was a rendezvous point for all New Mexican caravans going to Missouri that season. There they banded together for protection from the Indians. Gurulé tells us that on that occasion the convoy numbered almost four hundred wagons and carts, plus a huge herd of reserve oxen and mules. For the New Mexican drovers, a crossing of the prairies in those days was a grueling ordeal. Some always died on the way, either from Indian fights or from disease. Mothers and wives left behind would light candles in their mens' absence and lock the family saint in a wooden chest. If the men got back safely, the saint was taken out and honored with singing and dancing. But if news came that a loved one had perished on the trail, then the saint was removed from the chest and buried.

In Indian country and on stretches without water, the caravan traveled eighteen hours a day without stopping, to make extra time. Often José Gurulé, who walked beside a wagon and prodded the oxen with a pole, had to jog to keep up. The men were allowed only one full meal during each twenty-four hours, he tells us. But they got two light snacks, consisting of a tortilla and an onion, which had to be eaten on the run. And he adds, "The army of hirelings traveled on its feet with very little assistance from its stomach." All suffered from lack of sleep, and it was not uncommon for drovers to doze off while they were walking. On the march one man tried to steal a nap by stretching out on a wagon tongue. Once asleep he fell off and was trampled to death by the oxen. His companions held a hasty funeral and went on.

At the end of three months, the convoy reached Kansas City and went into camp on the outskirts. Here was more work for the scarecrow-thin drovers, as they had to unload the wool, deliver it to warehouses, and then begin preparations for the return homeward. Some of the wagons took on merchandise such as kettles, cutlery, china, bolts of cloth, and clothing for José Leandro Perea. But since these goods were less bulky than the wool, other wagons went home empty.

Gurulé and some of his friends from Las Placitas slipped away from the campground to go sight-seeing. To young fellows from rural New Mexico, the wonders of Kansas City were almost too much to be believed. On one street they were attracted by the sound of music to a large theater. In front stood a minstrel band, the performers dressed in white coats and pants and tall black hats.

The New Mexicans stood about with their mouths hanging open, too poor to pay the price of admission. José had some money in his pocket, obtained before he left home by selling several of his goats. But he intended to buy a worsted suit—that had been his dream for months—and he was not about to spend a cent on minstrel shows.

The stay in Kansas City was short. The men had arrived in tatters, almost barefoot and naked. So wagon master Esquipulo Romero outfitted them with new garments. But he carefully entered the costs in the Perea ledger alongside each recipient's name, to be charged against his salary. No charity here!

The landing at Kansas City as it would have appeared to José Gurulé in 1867. (from *Harper's Weekly*, 1897)

Heading back the great convoy reached the Arkansas River in central Kansas, where it split. Esquipulo Romero and some of the other wagon bosses had heard that the Kansas Pacific was laying track three days to the north, at Hays City, and was hiring teamsters. So they cut the empty wagons from the train and sent them up to work for the railroad. The boy José Gurulé was delighted with conditions he found in the rail camp. In contrast to the scanty rations the New Mexicans had been used to, they were now given white bread and butter, ham, bacon, fresh meat, coffee, and all the sugar cubes they wanted. Best of all they got three regular meals a day. But no wages did they see. Those were collected from the railroad by Romero and added to the account of José Leandro Perea.

At last the work was completed, and the men were bound for New Mexico once more. At Cold Spring, a famous Santa Fe Trail stop in the Oklahoma Panhandle, cholera broke out. A halt had to be called for twelve days, for not enough drovers were on their feet to keep the caravan moving. A mixture of whiskey and red chili was given to the sick as medicine, but not surprisingly it failed to cure. José and a few others who avoided falling ill were kept busy with shovels digging graves. The wagons took up the march again, creeping slowly and making frequent rest or burial stops. In December they reached Las Vegas and soon afterward were in Las Placitas. The round-trip had taken almost eleven months.

The train was disbanded and the men paid off. Each received $8 as his entire wage! For the work in the railroad camps, they got nothing, for as Esquipulo Romero explained, the rich food they had eaten there was compensation enough. Nothing was said about paying the $8 to the families of the men who had died of cholera.

For all the hardships and perils, young José Gurulé, who had turned seventeen on the trail, was satisfied with his year of labor. From Kansas City he had brought home a suit of worsted cloth. When he put it on and strutted about the plaza, the whole village turned out to see him. It was the first suit of clothes ever worn in Las Placitas.

21

A DREADFUL MASSACRE

AFTER 130 YEARS America's Civil War still grips the public imagination. The drama and tragedy were so profound, the bloodletting so liberal, that the four-year-long conflict left a permanent imprint upon the national psyche.

An interesting aspect of the war is that a number of generals on both sides had seen service in the Southwest during their formative years. One was General James Longstreet, Lee's second in command at Gettysburg, who had been stationed at Albuquerque in the 1850s.

General Ambrose E. Burnside, named by Lincoln in 1862 to command the Army of the Potomac, was another who got his military feet wet in New Mexico. Indeed as a young officer, just shortly out of West Point and garrisoned at Las Vegas, New Mexico, he became involved in a tragic episode on the old Santa Fe Trail.

As a fuzz-faced lieutenant, Burnside was known among his men for telling obscene stories and singing ribald songs. That does not seem to have affected his later reputation, for after the Civil War he became governor of Rhode Island and a U.S. senator.

In mid-May of 1850, a caravan of merchants out of Santa Fe passed through Las Vegas on its way east to Missouri. Much to the astonishment of Burnside and the other soldiers, the train suddenly rolled back into town the following week, with a grisly tale to tell. The party had gotten as far as Wagon Mound, a prominent landmark on the Santa Fe Trail, alongside today's I-25, about midway between El Paso and Denver. There according to one of the merchants, "we beheld a shocking sight."* Scattered upon the ground were the arrow-riddled bodies of ten men who had been accompanying the westbound mail wagon from Ft. Leavenworth. Wolves and ravens had partially devoured the corpses. The Indian attackers cut open the leather mail bags, and letters were strewn across the prairie, some of them skewered on yuccas. Thoroughly frightened, the merchants abandoned their intention of going on and instead fled back to Las Vegas to notify the authorities.

Lieutenant Burnside was ordered by his superior to take a troop and go to the massacre site, there to bury the victims and attempt to learn the identity of the culprits. Arriving at the Wagon Mound, Burnside easily found the wrecked mail wagon and the bodies, "in a complete state of putrification." His men collected them for mass burial.

The lieutenant walked over the battlefield and picked up numerous arrows. His scout identified them as belonging to

---

*Philadelphia Ledger, July 2, 1850.

Ambrose E. Burnside, as he appeared at the time of the Civil War. (author's collection)

the Jicarilla Apaches and Utes, two allied tribes who had lately been conducting raids along the trail. From the signs Burnside read that day and from information later given by Jicarilla Chief Chacón, the story of the massacre can be pieced together.

Profile of Wagon Mound, New Mexico. (photo by Evelyn Vinogradov)

The attack had actually begun twenty miles northeast of the Wagon Mound, at the crossing of the Canadian River. An Apache war party set an ambush for the mail wagon there, but the whites fought their way through and made a gallant dash for the Wagon Mound. A running skirmish lasted all day, during which two of the men received arrows in the thigh, a common battle injury for those on horseback. At dusk the mail party reached the foot of the Mound and went into camp. The members were no doubt hoping that their strategy of staying on the move would see them through to safety on the following day.

Unfortunately during the night the Apaches were joined by a large band of Utes, who taunted them, saying, "You Jicarillas don't know how to fight Americans, so we will show you in the morning." At dawn the Indians, who now numbered more than one hundred, struck the mailmen. They offered stout resistence, but within a short time they were overcome and slain.

In his official report of the episode, Lieutenant Burnside wrote: "So large a party of Americans have never before been entirely destroyed by the Indians. Ten Americans have heretofore been considered comparatively safe in traveling over the trail."* The Indians were never punished for this specific crime. But one result was the building of Ft. Union (1851) a few miles from the Wagon Mound, to protect traffic to and from Santa Fe.

As for Ambrose Burnside, he is best remembered now for popularizing the wearing of side-whiskers. The style was first known as "burnsides," but was later inverted to become "sideburns."

---

*Annie Heloise Abel, *The Official Correspondence of James S. Calhoun* (Washington, GPO, 1915), 198–99.

22

FLYING THE SANTA FE TRAIL

WHEN IT COMES to air travel, there are two kinds of people: those who enjoy flying in small planes, and those who do not. I am, unquestionably, a member of the second category. Walking barefoot across a rocky field inhabited by rattlesnakes is easier for me than climbing into a pint-sized aircraft and winging into the skies. I explained that very carefully to pilot Michael Heller, when he agreed to fly me in his light plane from Santa Fe to the Point of Rocks in southwestern Kansas, following the ruts of the Santa Fe Trail. "Nothing to it," he chuckled. "You'll love every minute of it." I could see that he did not take my professed aversion to flying very seriously.

My misgivings grew at the first glimpse of Heller's tiny craft parked in front of the Santa Fe Air Terminal. "It's made of aluminum and weighs only 1600 pounds," he told me. "Sound as a dollar!" Swallowing a couple of pills to prevent air sickness, I slid into the narrow bucket seat and fastened the belt. As we soared into the blue autumn sky, the pilot yelled above the clamor of the motor, "This'll be the easiest trip you've ever made."

As soon as we were airborne, I began peering earthward, looking for signs of the old trail that, after 1821, had become New Mexico's main highway of commerce leading from the Missouri frontier. The first few minutes were disappointing. The trail evidently had followed closely the present route of Interstate 25 and the Santa Fe Railroad tracks, which parallel each other for much of the sixty-five miles between Santa Fe and Las Vegas. Building the highway and the rail line had disturbed so much land that trail remains have all but vanished. Michael was beginning to think we were on a wild-goose chase. So, I shouted to him: "Don't worry. We'll pick it up as soon as we get on the plains beyond Las Vegas." And we did just that.

Approaching Watrous, the bold, clear ruts of the Santa Fe Trail rose to view, engraved indelibly in the unbroken prairie sod. Michael was as excited as I was. In past days, Watrous was known as La Junta, the "Meeting Place," because at that point the two main branches of the trail coming from the east united and continued as a single road toward New Mexico's capital. The longer leg, called the Mountain Branch, followed the Arkansas Valley through western Kansas and into Colorado, where it angled down through Raton Pass and skirted the foot of the mountains to La Junta. The other route, known as the Cimarron Cutoff, left the Arkansas in central Kansas and headed toward New Mexico in a more direct line. It was 100 miles shorter that way, but water was scarce and the Indians more troublesome.

Junction of the Mountain Branch and Cimarron Cutoff at the Sapello Stage Station, near modern Watrous, New Mexico. (author's collection)

I instructed Michael to fly eastward along the Cimarron Cutoff, which leads past the Wagon Mound and the Rabbit Ears, famous landmarks familiar to early travelers. Most of the way the trail crosses undisturbed rangeland, and I knew we would have no trouble staying on course.

North of Clayton we crossed into the Oklahoma Panhandle and came upon the twisting bed of the Cimarron River. It contained only gleaming white sand, no water. Nor did it have any water 150 years ago, when ox-drawn caravans passed by. Then thirsty men and women would dig a hole in the dry bed, let a small pool seep in, and take a drink. One disgruntled wayfarer declared in his journal that the scant water

Kearny Gap, center, on the Santa Fe Trail, near Las Vegas, New Mexico, upper left. Deeply eroded trail ruts fill the valley at lower left. (author's collection)

was so heavy with alkali and chalky white that it made an excellent substitute for milk. But foul as the liquid may have been, most people were glad to get it.

Once out of New Mexico, the trail ruts, seen from the air, became steadily more elusive. Plowed fields now were common, and wherever the farmer's tractor had turned the soil, furrows laid down by pioneer freight wagons disappeared. Our plane left Oklahoma, sliced the extreme southeast corner of Colorado, and dipped into Kansas. There we caught sight of Middle Spring at Point of Rocks, a well-known campsite and one of the rare sources of fresh water along the Cimarron Cutoff. Stretching beyond was a solid patchwork of grain fields. So I suggested to Michael that we turn around and head for Raton, where we could pick up the section of the Mountain Branch that led back to Watrous. Below Raton we spotted a tiny airfield and landed to gas up. The single short runway was filled with chuckholes, and Michael jerked us from side to side trying to miss them. At a lone fuel pump standing in the middle of the prairie next to a trailer, a man waited to fill our tank.

"Where you headed," he asked.

"We're following the ruts of the Santa Fe Trail," I replied. "You get many trail hounds stopping by here?"

"Not many," he answered. "In fact, I do believe you're the first ones."

Airborne again, our little silver plane easily found the Mountain Branch and pursued its sharp track past Cimarron, past Kit Carson's old home at Rayado, and down through some isolated mesas that pointed toward Fort Union. Updrafts from the Sangre de Cristo Mountains on our right sent us bouncing, and I began to turn green. When I complained of the turbulence, Michael insisted that we were experiencing nothing more than minor ripples.

Surrounding the ghostly ruins of Fort Union, now a National Monument, we encountered the greatest concentration of trail ruts seen thus far. Founded in 1851 to protect passing caravans and also to serve as the main supply depot for other posts in New Mexico, Fort Union hummed with intense activity for almost three decades. Practically everyone who played an important role in the early history of the Territory stopped by here.

Shortly thereafter we reached the "Meeting Place" at Watrous again and retraced our flight path back to Santa Fe. In five and one-half hours of air travel, I had followed portions of the Santa Fe Trail that had once taken the wagonmasters weeks to cover. The telescoping of time, made possible by the machine age, was something those hardy frontiersmen could never have conceived of.

"Now wasn't that a great trip, like I promised you?" Michael Heller asked. "I wouldn't be surprised if you want me to do it again sometime."

And I replied with the greatest sincerity: "I wouldn't have missed it. But I'll guarantee you that the next time I go over the trail, it won't be by airplane. I don't like those ripples. I'm going by wagon!"

23

THE INN AT THE
END OF THE TRAIL

Among the many historical landmarks of New Mexico's capital city, La Fonda occupies a conspicuous place. A sign over the entrance proudly proclaims it to be the "Inn at the End of the Trail." For more than 150 years, this hostelry has remained the favorite lodging for travelers arriving on the Santa Fe Trail.

The exact origins of La Fonda are a bit obscure. There is reason to believe that some sort of inn existed on the site in the days when New Mexico was a province of Spain. The Camino Real, or "King's Road," ran past the front door and stretched southward to El Paso and beyond. The Camino, at least that part of it in downtown Santa Fe, is now called San Francisco Street, after the town's patron saint. Later when the Santa Fe Trail was in full swing, the hotel was operated by a Missouri couple, William and Mary Donoho (until 1837). Afterward it became a popular rendezvous for pioneer merchants, Indian traders, trappers, and soldiers. Everyone called it simply "La Fonda Americana," implying "The hotel where all the Americans stayed." Some early guests claimed that as to service and quality of meals, it ranked second only to the palatial Planter's House in St. Louis.

In those days I suspect it was La Fonda's large gambling hall that proved its biggest drawing card. There were billiard tables and tables for poker and Mexican monte. Another favorite game was *chusas,* similar to roulette. The play was loud, wild, and sometimes ended in gunsmoke. Several of the guest rooms facing the street were rented to private parties who wished to play for high stakes in a quieter atmosphere. The management provided a bountiful supply of liquor and cigars at no charge. That custom has fallen by the wayside, and of course, gambling is no longer allowed.

When General Stephen Watts Kearny arrived with his conquering army in 1846, he threw a large ball in La Fonda's main hall to celebrate the taking of New Mexico by the United States. Reports say the room was draped with colorful banners and that dignitaries from as far away as Taos, Socorro, and El Paso were in attendance. Soon afterward a pair of new owners, Frank Green and Thomas Bowler, took charge of the hotel. They called it the Exchange Hotel, but many people continued to use the old name. Green took a trip south to Chihuahua City to hire new help. He brought back two expert bartenders, a half dozen experienced waiters, and a musical group called Pancho's Band that featured an accomplished harpist. These employees added more luster to the hotel's reputation.

Unfortunately the violence of the day often intruded. A

San Francisco Street in Santa Fe, with La Fonda on the right. (Museum of New Mexico, negative no. 31339)

young soldier drinking at the bar in 1851 tells us that a stranger entered one evening, downed a whiskey, then pulled a pistol and commenced firing at random. Several people were struck, including a lawyer shot in the stomach. Upon being arrested, the assailant claimed his actions were justified. Said he: "A friend of mine from Texas was killed in Santa Fe and all the inhabitants of the town are cut-throats, robbers, and murderers." He too was a Texan. Later that night he was taken from the jail by friends of the lawyer and hanged in the backyard of the Exchange. The yard is now occupied by La Fonda's covered dining patio.

Even more sensational was the killing in 1867 of Chief

Justice John Slough, of the Territorial Supreme Court. He was gunned down in the Exchange lobby by W. L. Rynerson, the legislative representative from Las Cruces. It was said a political disagreement led to the tragedy.

Over the years many famous persons signed the Exchange's guest register. Among them were all the territorial governors, Kit Carson, Josiah Gregg, Archbishop John B. Lamy, Sheriff Pat Garrett, and a couple of U.S. presidents. Billy the Kid, while not a guest, is said to have washed dishes in the hotel kitchen. But that seems a bit farfetched. Once a Mr. Jones from St. Louis checked in and soon fell gravely ill. The proprietors neglected him badly, making no attempt to call a doctor. Three days later the chamber maid reported that Mr. Jones was dead in his bed. A search through his papers revealed, to everyone's astonishment, that he had been extremely wealthy. Suddenly there was a flurry of activity to arrange an appropriate funeral. But while he was being prepared for the coffin, Mr. Jones came to life again, having merely been in a temporary coma.

Someone asked Mr. Jones what it was like to have "died." In reply he recalled having passed a great distance, where he arrived at the Gates of Heaven. St. Peter was there and wanted to know where he had breathed his last. Mr. Jones answered that he had died in a place called Santa Fe, New Mexico. But St. Peter would not believe him, saying, "There's no such place. At least I've never heard of it." An atlas of the United States was then called for, and Mr. Jones pointed to Santa Fe on the map. "Sure enough, you are right," admitted St. Peter.

"But I'll be blest if you aren't the first man ever to come here from that town." At the completion of the story, no one asked Mr. Jones any more questions.

In the early part of this century, the Exchange went into decline and was finally closed. But during the 1920s, it was completely rebuilt in the Pueblo-Spanish style and assumed its original name, La Fonda. Until 1969 it was one of the famous Harvey Houses associated with the Santa Fe Railroad.

Today the La Fonda continues the grand traditions of the past. Those who are fortunate enough to pass a night under its roof rub shoulders with the ghosts of men and women who once made history in the Southwest.

ᴬᴬᴬᴬᴬ ACKNOWLEDGMENTS ᴬᴬᴬᴬᴬ

Aʟʟ ᴏꜰ ᴛʜᴇ material in this book was originally published in journals or periodicals and is reprinted here with permission, in those few cases in which the author is not the holder of the copyright.

The three opening chapters appeared serially under the title "The Old Trail to Santa Fe," in the quarterly of the Oregon-California Trails Association, *Overland Journal,* the spring, summer, and fall issues (vol. 4, 2–4), 1986.

Sources for the essays in part II are as follows: "Whither Becknell!" was privately printed in pamphlet form by the author in 1971 and reprinted in the *Westport Historical Quarterly* 7(2) (June 1971), under the title "Opening the Santa Fe Trail." "The Santa Fe Trail as High Adventure" was delivered as the opening address at the Santa Fe Trail Association Symposium, Hutchinson, Kansas, September 25, 1987, and was published, with some minor changes, in Leo E. Oliva, ed., *Adventure on the Santa Fe Trail* (Topeka: Kansas State Historical Society, 1988).

"Pecos Pueblo on the Santa Fe Trail" initially saw light in David Grant Noble, ed., *Pecos Ruins* (Santa Fe: School of American Research, 1981). Two essays are drawn from the quarterly of the Santa Fe Trail Association, *Wagon Tracks*. They are "Bernard Seligman: Jewish Merchant," 3(1) (November 1988), and "Comets and Meteors," 5(3) (May 1991). Finally "The Poetry of the Santa Fe Trail" was given as a lecture at the Santa Fe Trail Association Symposium, Trinidad, Colorado, September 12, 1986, and subsequently published in David N. Wetzel, ed., *The Santa Fe Trail: New Perspectives* (Denver: Colorado Historical Society, 1987).

The sketches in part III were published on various dates between 1979 and 1991 in the following periodicals: *El Paso Times, Santa Fe Reporter, Socorro Defensor-Chieftain,* and *Boise City* [OK] *News.*

═════ BIBLIOGRAPHICAL ═════
NOTE

ALL RESEARCH ON the Santa Fe Trail must begin with reference to Jack D. Rittenhouse's monumental work, *The Santa Fe Trail: A Historical Bibliography* (Albuquerque: University of New Mexico Press, 1971). Issued to commemorate the 150th anniversary of the opening of the trail, the volume was long out of print, commanding as much as $75 on the rare book market. In 1986, however, the author brought out a facsimile reprint in a quality paperback. Also useful is Marc Simmons, "Women on the Santa Fe Trail: Diaries, Journals, Memoirs—An Annotated Bibliography," *New Mexico Historical Review* 61 (July 1986): 233–43.

All books listed here represent titles that have appeared since Rittenhouse's bibliography in 1971. His compilation embraced 718 entries; in the twenty-five years that have followed, at least one hundred new works have been published. Only a few of the most significant can be included in this brief summary.

A single new general history of the trail made its appearance. It is Seymour V. Connor and Jimmy M. Skaggs, *Broadcloth and Britches: The Santa Fe Trade* (College Station: Texas A&M University Press, 1977). Another highly useful volume, of sterling merit, is Louise Barry, *The Beginning of the West* (Topeka: Kansas State Historical Society, 1972). In the form of a chronology, it quotes newspapers (printed through 1854) with regard to activities on western trails. It must be considered a prime sourcebook.

Among newly printed firsthand journals and recollections of trail life, the following are particularly noteworthy: Lina Fergusson Browne, ed., *Trader on the Santa Fe Trail: Memoirs of Franz Huning* (Albuquerque: Calvin Horn Publisher, 1973); Robert W. Frazier, ed., *Over the Chihuahua and Santa Fe Trails, 1847–1848: George Rutledge Gibson's Journal* (Albuquerque: University of New Mexico Press, 1981); and David K. Strate, ed., *West by Southwest: Letters of Joseph Pratt Allyn, a Traveler along the Santa Fe Trail, 1863* (Dodge City: Kansas Heritage Center, 1984). A dozen brief original narratives and reminiscences are printed in Marc Simmons, ed., *On the Santa Fe Trail* (Lawrence: University Press of Kansas, 1986). Recent additions to the literature are Barton H. Barbour, ed., *Reluctant Frontiersman: James Ross Larkin on the Santa Fe Trail, 1856–57* (Albuquerque: University of New Mexico Press, 1990); and Mark L. Gardner, ed., *Brothers on the Santa Fe and Chihuahua Trails* (Niwot: University Press of Colorado, 1993).

Several new biographies have shed light on the careers of persons prominently associated with the trail. First in importance is Larry M. Beachum's *William Becknell: Father of the Santa Fe Trade* (El Paso: Texas Western Press, 1982). Donald Chaput did a fine job with his much needed biography of *François X. Aubry: Trader, Trailmaker and Voyageur in the Southwest, 1846–1854* (Glendale, CA: Arthur H. Clark Co., 1975). Another significant figure, who built a fort at La Junta, New Mexico, modeled after that of the Bents, at last receives recognition in George P. Hammond's *The Adventures of Alexander Barclay, Mountain Man* (Denver: Old West Publishing Co., 1976). Activities of the Hardemans in the early Santa Fe trade are described in Nicholas Perkins Hardeman, *Wilderness Calling* (Knoxville: University of Tennessee Press, 1977). See too Marian Meyer, *Mary Donoho: New First Lady of the Santa Fe Trail* (Santa Fe: Ancient City Press, 1991); and Thomas E. Chávez, *Manuel Alvarez, 1794–1856* (Niwot: University Press of Colorado, 1990).

Four important titles on forts are Leo E. Oliva, *Fort Union and the Frontier Army in the Southwest* (Santa Fe: National Park Service, 1993); Leo E. Oliva, *Fort Larned on the Santa Fe Trail* (Topeka: Kansas State Historical Society, 1982); Rhoda Woodridge, *Fort Osage* (Independence, MO: Independence Press, 1983); and Enid Thompson et al., *Bent's Old Fort* (Colorado Springs: Williams Printing, 1979). A welcome contribution to the military history is William Y. Chalfant, *Dangerous Passage: The Santa Fe Trail and the Mexican War* (Norman: University of Oklahoma Press, 1994).

For those wishing to retrace the trail on the ground, the following books will provide assistance: Gene and Mary Martin, *Trail Dust* (Boulder: Johnson Books, 1972); and the second, revised and expanded edition of Marc Simmons, *Following the Santa Fe Trail* (Santa Fe: Ancient City Press, 1986). Not to be missed are two basic titles by Gregory M. Franzwa: *The Santa Fe Trail Revisited* (St. Louis: Patrice Press, 1989) and *Maps of the Santa Fe Trail* (St. Louis: Patrice Press, 1989).